To All Those Who Seek Truth

A Compilation of Bhagavan Sri Sathya
Sai Baba's Divine Discourses

Approved and Signed by Baba August 9th 1999

ॐ

50% of the proceeds from the sale of this book will
be donated to those in need, supporting the work of
Sri Sathya Sai Baba Seva in Africa.

Photographs relating to this publication stem from several historical and
uniquely personal experiences relating to the author, and in the Divine
Presence (Darshan) of *Bhagavan Sri Sathya Sai Baba*. As such there is a
lack of uniformity of photographic clarity, which might otherwise be
expected in a published book. It is widely considered to be more valuable
to share in the precious recalling of such events, in a way that points to
the integrity of the content of the book, to add to the readers experience.

Layout by Karl Hunt

ISBN 9798300083878

BHAGAVAN SRI SATHYA SAI BABA

AMRITHA

THE NECTAR OF IMMORTALITY

"Whoever Reads This Book is Blessed"
– Baba

Compiled by Obou Roger Digbo

ACKNOWLEDGMENTS

This special compilation of *Bhagavan Sri Sathya Sai Baba's* Divine Discourses has come into being with the help of various people, over several years since Baba first signed and blessed it. Firstly, I want to particularly thank my beloved wife Maggy, who has always been my backbone of support along with our children Marie-Caroline, Hari, Jean Michael, and Pierre Emanuel. Even when the children were at a very young age, they were always by my side, helping me with typing, and compiling discourses, and we had many happy family discussions on these topics in study circles, which often also included my brothers, Lambert, Gregoire, Patrick, and Opape. This was our foundation for Human Values Classes, and is the Divine Gift of *Our Lord, Bhagavan Sri Sathya Sai Baba.*

As we were planning to go to *Prasanthi Nilayam*, our daughter Marie Caroline (aged 13 years at the time), urged me to bring the manuscript version of this book with us, confidently saying: *"Dad, take the book to Baba, He will sign it, even if it's not fully finished"*. That is exactly what happened when *Baba* called us together for an interview on August 9th, 1999, and signed and blessed it. I would like to thank a good friend Valerie Marion, and her husband, as some years ago Valerie originally typed some initial chapters. Thanks also to Marie and Dominique Didier and Nathalie and Jean-Eric M'doihama and their families. Eric, (my younger brother), always encouraged and supported me in creating this book. My special thanks also go to SaraSai Woods, a very good friend, and *Sai* devotee living in London, who saw the global importance of these precious discourses. Being a writer, she strongly encouraged me to commit to publishing this English version of *Amritha,* offering her service in editing, preparing, and publishing the content.

Baba, We Love You
Baba, We Love You
Baba, We Love You
Om Sairam – Om Sairam – Om Sairam

Roger Digbo

This compilation of *Bhagavan Sri Sathya Sai Baba's* Discourses was signed and approved by *Baba* during an Interview with the author Obou Roger Digbo at *Prasanthi Nilayam*, Puttaparthi, August 9th, 1999.

OMSAIRAM

LOVE ALL SERVE ALL, HELP EVER HURT NEVER

AUTHOR'S INTRODUCTION

This compilation of *Bhagavan Sri Sathya Sai Baba's* Discourses entitled ***Amritha – The Nectar of Immortality*** was originally written in French and blessed by *Bhagavan Sri Sathya Sai Baba* during a private interview in Prasanthi Nilayam, Puttaparthi, India on August 9th, 1999, at which time Baba approved, blessed, and signed it.

During a private interview, as I knelt at His Divine Lotus Feet, *Baba* asked: "*Where is My Book?* "As any of *Baba's* Devotees know, such a Divine Blessing provides the much sought-after green light to proceed in any endeavor, fully confident in *Baba's* guidance and direction, according to His Divine Will. With the book in His Hands, as He looked through the con- tents, *Baba* further enquired "*What is your mother tongue?*" to which I replied "*Bhete*". (This is one of the native languages of Ivory Coast, West Africa). *Baba* then stated clearly "*Translate this into your mother tongue.*" and signed it on the spot, while pronouncing the following powerful statement: "*Whoever Reads This Book is Blessed.*"

As I look around me in the current situation in worldly events, it has become clear to me that His Words of Loving Truth and Eternal Guidance are desperately needed to bring comfort to all who have the heart to listen. It could literally be described as Divine food for the soul. As I cannot think of eating this Celestial Prasad (Divine Food) alone, it feels important for me to share it, so that many more people will benefit from this assured blessing.

I have paid particular attention to the order of the following chapters, as together we follow His Divine Messages on a journey of discovery of the true meaning of our temporal sojourn in this transient worldly existence.

Every single word uttered by *Baba* is *Divine Amritha*, the nectar of immortality. Even the highest celestial beings and Angels yearn for this precious medicine administered by *Bhagavan Sri Sathya Sai Baba* (our Divine Father/Mother) for our ailing hearts. Once taken, it leads us into Self-Realization, and the knowing that we are Divine Embodiments of Love, eternally protected in his Loving care.

I leave you to discover for yourself His Life, and His Divine Message in the following chapters, and in doing so, to graduate from the Spiritual Academy of Humanity to the culmination of our human destiny. Focus strongly on the Name that Redeems all souls and awaken to the Divine potential promised by Him to all, as our innate birth right:

Om Sairam, Om Sairam, Om Sairam

THE INCOMPARABLE MAJESTY AND
MYSTERY OF THIS UNIQUE SAI

Dear Friends!

Today for the first time in human history, the world is thrilling with joy, awakening in the Light, full of Love and transported to Heaven by a phenomenon in human form; Bhagavan Sri Sathya Sai Baba, the Embodiment of Love, Wisdom, and Power, whose Omnipresence is experienced by all human beings of all continents, of all colors, of all beliefs, whatever their languages, their standard of living and culture. Millions of people have seen His charming silhouette and have heard His soothing voice. Countless people have adopted His Message as a source of light to guide their steps. By His Grace, many of His people were healed of their physical, mental, and intellectual suffering. Many spiritual seekers found in Him the goal they so desired. It is therefore not surprising that a large number of people in each country feel the ardent desire to share this immense Joy that he dispenses, to receive the Light that he offers. To welcome the Love that he offers in their hearts, is to respond to His call, to realize that God is within us. They are very anxious to know how and where to find the Savior who comes for them. Writings and rosaries, photos and presents, icons and incense used in their worship, are weak instruments to measure the incommensurable majesty and mystery of this unique Sai. So, doubt and incredulity, hesitation and fear, haunt the pilgrims until the end of the journey. This book I believe will, like a friend or sympathetic companion, help the sincere and serious seeker to wake up, to rise up, and to continue on his way.

Professor Narasimha Kasturi
Biographer of Bhagavan Sri Sathya Sai Baba

Here is the human form in which each Divine Entity, each Divine Principle, that is to say, all the Names and all the Forms attributed to God by man, have manifested themselves. Do not be distracted by doubt. If you install in the bottom of your heart a strong faith in My Reality as Sarva Daivatha Swarupam, that is to say, the Incarnation of all Forms of God, you will soon have a Vision of My Reality"
            Bhagavan Sri Sathya Sai Baba.

MESSAGE OF LOVE

FROM BHAGAVAN SRI SATHYA SAI BABA

"I have come", He says "To wake you all,
You, who sleep the sleep of ages . . .
While one by one the pages
Of account book of paltry deeds and thoughts
Accumulate in defiling piles . . . and keep you from
the happy land, Above, beyond the sleep,
the dream, above, beyond the waking stage . . .
The realm of restful supreme peace"

"I have come", He says, to save you all,
You, who stray in silly pride,
Hunting fantasies in bush and briar
with bandaged eyes in pitch dark gloom
and fall into birth and death,
Failure, fracture, faction, fanatic fire"

"I have come", He says, to cure you all . . .
From petty selfish inanities!
Trivial tinsel temporalities
Your tweedledums and tweedledees,
The little loves and hates, peevish paisa rivalries
Across dividing line of 'mine' and 'thine'!
Brother gouging brothers' eye
Sister crushing sister's babe –
because of the sin of the wall that separates them!"

"I have come", He says, to show you all
The Path, the Form, the Name, the Way of Life
That cools and calms the fevered Mind,
That stills the waves,
That fills, fulfils.
That leads you into He (whom you forgot,)
That follows you into that from which you came"

Here you can find on every page
The Words He spoke for You.
A few which I dared translate
into uncouth English tongue . . .
The few I gathered from His lips
As I sat at The Feet to catch His Voice
So sweet, so charged with Grace!

The solar rays, they open wide
The buds of Lotus, waiting for the warmth!
May Baba's Words, their warning touch
Unfurl the petals of your lotus heart!

Professor Narayana Kasturi 16-09-1963

SSSSSSSSSSSSSSSSSSSSSSSSSSSSSSSSSSSSSSSSSSSSSSSSSSSSSSS
DIVINE DISCOURSES
SSSSSSSSSSSSSSSSSSSSSSSSSSSSSSSSSSSSSSSSSSSSSSSSSSSSSSS

Bhagavan's Divine Messages of Love for Everyone

1

WHO AM I?

The Cosmos is a manifestation of God. Foolish are they, who while seeing the handiwork of God everywhere, think that there is no God. Without recognizing the Omnipresence of God, man seeks God somewhere or other. This reflects the dualistic attitude of people who identify themselves with the body and alienate themselves from God. While God is Omnipresent and can be recognized in the Divine Manifestations of Nature, body consciousness prevents man from experiencing Oneness with God.

HOW IS GOD TO BE EXPERIENCED?

How is God to be experienced? The first pre-requisite is purity of heart. All religions have affirmed the basic importance of purity. The aim of all Sadhanas (spiritual efforts) is to achieve Peace. Compassion towards all beings is devotion to God. God cannot be obtained through the ostentatious observance of rituals and worship. Where there is pomp and show, there can be no Divinity. The Bliss of the Divine cannot be found there. As a seed will not sprout on rocky ground, the Bliss of God cannot be realized by worship devoid of humility and sincerity.

THE PURPOSE OF ALL SADHANAS

All *Sadhanas* (spiritual efforts) are not pursued for realizing the *Atma*. There is no need to seek the *Atma*, which is all pervasive and present everywhere. *Sadhanas* are performed to get rid of the *Anatma* (that which bars the vision of the *Atma*). Man forgets his real nature and loses himself in the consciousness of what he is not. He forgets that he is the *Atma* in reality.

In the state of deep sleep, one is totally unaware of his name, form, position etc. On waking, however, he realizes, that the 'I' of which he is conscious in the waking state, was present in deep sleep also. The purpose of all *Sadhana* is to discover the nature of the 'I' that is experienced in all the different states of waking, dreaming and deep sleep.

THE ATMA (SOUL) IS THE BASIS FOR EVERYTHING

In the waking state, man identifies himself with a particular name and form and builds up all relations on that basis, but how real and permanent are these names and forms? They are all projections of the mind and have an existence only as long as the body and mind remain. The heart represents the *Atma* (*Soul*). It is self-effulgent. The light from the heart '*Atma*' illumines the mind and enables it to see the external world. Without this illumination, the mind cannot comprehend the world. The mind is like the moon which receives its light from the sun. It has no light of its own. It shines because of the light from the *Atma*. When the sun shines,

2

the moon is hardly visible. Likewise, when there is awareness of the *Atma*, the mind is not perceivable. The *Soul* is the basis for everything.

Men are naïve in imagining that the *Atma* is in the body. The truth is, the body, the mind, the entire cosmos, is in the *Atma*. The *Atma* cannot be inside anything else. It is the All. It is Everything. Those who perform *Japa, Dhyana,* or *Pooja* conceiving God as separate from themselves, are victims of the delusion of dualism. Whatever their scholarship, they are ignorant of their own true nature when they alienate God from themselves. God is the very heart of man.

All man's spiritual exercises are at the mental level. By these means the *Atma* cannot be realized. The Vedas have declared:

'*Yatho vacho nivarthanthe aprapya manasasaha*'

'*Whence mind and speech turn back unable to reach it*'
Neither the mind nor speech can comprehend the nature of the *Atma*. The mind is turned towards the external by the sense organs. It is only by withdrawing it from sense objects, that the mind can be made to develop *Antarmukham* which is (the Inner Vision).

THE ESSENTIAL OBJECTIVE OF ALL SPIRITUAL QUESTS

The 'I' Principle is present everywhere. It began with God alone. The first word was '*Aham*' '*I*'. Even the *Pranava*' *Om*' came after '*Aham*'. Before all creation, '*Aham*' alone existed. That '*Aham*' became the many. One who realizes the Oneness of what he regards as his '*I*' with the Cosmic '*Aham*' alone knows his reality. The Universal '*I*' appears under different names and forms in different bodies related to time and circumstance. Even the same person goes through many changes in form and relationships in life, but the 'I' remains unchanged. It is like an actor wearing different disguises while himself remaining one and the same. The realization of the unchanging and universal character of the '*I*' (the *Atma*) is the essential objective of the spiritual quest.

THE SOUL IS THE OMNIPRESENT & IMMUTABLE PRINCIPLE

The sense of duality arises when the '*I*' (*Aham*) assumes a specific form and name. '*Ahamkara*' (the *Ego-sense*) is the result of this change in form. It is only when man dissociates himself from name and form, that he can discover his true Divine Self. *To forget his essential Divinity and identify himself with a changing and impermanent form is the cause of all bondage and sorrow.* It is the mind that is the cause of this wrongful identification because of its involvement with the external world and the impressions received through the senses. When the workings of the mind are understood, the reality of the '*Atma*' which is beyond the mind, will be experienced as the One Omnipresent and Immutable Principle.

Duality is an obvious fact of everyday life. All *Sastras, Puranas* and *Ithihasas* (Epics) have recognized this duality and sought to regulate men's lives on that basis. As long as Men are engaged in activity in the phenomenal world in any capacity, the dualistic attitude is inescapable. All scriptural injunctions are designed to regulate man's conduct in the phenomenal and temporal world. The *Vedas* attach great importance to Time. The *Sastras* prescribe duties in relation to time, circumstance, and situation. The science of *Astrology* describes what should be done according to changes in time. The *Panchanga* (*Almanac*) indicates what is likely to happen on the basis of astrological data. During this New Year, *Prabhava*, the indications are encouraging. Out of the Nine '*Grahas*'(*Planets*) seven are favorably disposed. The Moon is the ruling planet for the year. *Kuja* (*Mars*) is the

Minister. Their influence is powerful in this year *Sani* (*Saturn*) is weak. There will be no scarcity of food or water this year. Food production will increase substantially.

THE REAL FRUIT OF AUSTERITIES

However beneficial the changes may be in the sphere of natural forces, without a change in man's mental outlook and conduct, they will be of no use. Many persons claim that they are observing rigorous austerities (*Tapas*). What is the outcome of these austerities? If their hearts soften and they show compassion towards the ailing and the helpless, only then has their penance any meaning. A compassion filled heart is the only real fruit of *Tapas*. All the *Sadhanas* performed by a hard-hearted person are utterly futile.

MEDITATION

Many undertake meditation as a spiritual exercise and expend many hours a day on it. But, in fact, meditation is implicit in almost every act that is done from morning till night. Meditation (in the sense of concentration), is implied in all the daily chores of eating, going to work, attending business, etc. One is meditating while reading or playing or shopping. Without concentration, no activity of any kind can be done. When the concentration is on God, it becomes spiritual meditation. Does this meditation call for any specific time or place? No, there is no special technique for meditation.

In giving meditation (*Dhyana*) some special names, they are forgetting its real significance. For instance, if people do not listen with *dhyana* (one pointed attention) to *Swami's Discourse*, they will not remember what *Swami* said. Even listening calls for dhyana. It has no specific form. No dhyana is possible with a wandering mind. Today, in the name of *Dhyana*, several stunts are being practiced. Instead of spending hours in so-called meditation with the mind restlessly hopping from one thought to another like a monkey, it would be better to concentrate on the performances of one's household's official and social duties, with earnestness and dedication. Is that not meditation?

Of what use is it to sit 'In meditation' for an hour, when you cannot keep your mind still for a minute? Think about God when carrying out your regular duties. Regard all work as a sacred offering to God. See God in everything you do. Instead of following this simple and easy path, people are engaging themselves in all gymnastics and subjecting themselves to various hazards. Devote yourselves to your duties. Meditation is not confined to any one thing. It should permeate every action you take.

THE REAL SOLITUDE

Some aspirants wish to seek *Ekantham* (*Solitude*) but being alone is not solitude. People go to *Hrishikesh, Haridwar,* or *Tapovanam,* in search of solitude. Only those who have not understood the real meaning of solitude will resort to such things. There is real *solitude* (*aloneness*) only when the mind is completely stilled. If while sitting alone in a forest your mind is ruminating on affairs of the world, how can it be called solitude? Without curbing thoughts, solitude cannot be found anywhere. Either thoughts have to be eliminated, or all thoughts should be turned to God.

Many imagine that they are deriving happiness by enjoying the things of the world. They should examine *who* is '*enjoying*' *whom*? In reality, far from enjoying the things they possess, it is their possessions which are enjoying them. The hatred, anger, envy, and other evils caused by possessions only lead to disease and misery. Why should the body suffer from ills if possessions were the source of happiness? Man is losing real happiness by attachment to things which cannot give him happiness.

SET YOUR SIGHT ON THE SUPREME

Those who have faith in the *Gita* (*Bhagavad Gita*) should note that it has clearly declared that this world is ephemeral and a *'Vale of Tears'* and enduring bliss and peace are not to be found by attachment to it. The source of lasting peace and happiness is within ourselves. That is the *Atma* (*the Omni-Self*). It is by realizing *'The Omni Self'* that peace and bliss have to be secured. One must constantly develop the consciousness that the *Atma* is everything, the *Doer*, the *Deed*, and the *Outcome* thereof. When the consciousness is broadened in this way, in due course it leads to *Self-Realization*. If your vision is broad, your destination will also be of the same magnitude. A narrow outlook can only lead to a narrow valley. If you are immersed all the time in the petty trifles of mundane existence, when will you ever understand the reality which is beyond the physical and the mental? Set your sight on the supreme. Then illumination will come in a flash.

DEVELOP THE CONSCIOUSNESS
"I AM ATMA"

Everyone should develop the consciousness, *"I am Atma, I am Brahman"*. When one says, *"I am Brahman"* it is evident that there is *"I"* in *Brahma*. Who is that *'I'*? *Brahma* means *Pervasiveness*. In declaring *"I am Brahman"*, the consciousness of *All-Pervasiveness* should be developed. *Brahman* is all pervasive. It is equally present everywhere. You should regard yourselves as *All Pervasive Omni-Self*. Whatever you do,

7

whatever you see, whatever you speak, saturate it with Divinity, so that you may be aware of your reality.

The world will exist for you as long as you have the feeling of duality. In the deep sleep state, you enjoy real bliss. You are not aware at that time of your body, your mind, your feelings, your qualities, your thoughts, but still *You* exist. That same pure *You* exists in the waking state, the dream state, and the deep-sleeping state. In the gross, the subtle and the causal states, *you* exist. In all these changing states and stages, it is the *Atmic Principle* which remains without undergoing any change.

THE ENQUIRY SHOULD GO ON AS THUS

The physical body which performs *Japam,* or *Dhyanam,* or the various other spiritual practices is but a water bubble. The mind which is based upon this physical body is but a mad monkey. With the help of this mad *monkey mind* and this *water-bubble body,* how can you hope to achieve the permanent *Atma? Japa, Dhyana, Bhajans,* austerities, sacrifices, these are all methods for temporarily controlling the mind. But there is one practice that will have a permanent effect, and that is enquiry. You should go on enquiring *"Who am I? Who am I?"* until you reach the stage where you find out who you really are. The enquiry should go on thus: *"Here is my body, here is my mind, my heart, my feelings, my intellect, my memory power. I am not any one of these! Someone has praised me; someone has censured me, but to whom does this pertain? Only to this physical body"* In this way you must develop a sense of detachment and a sacrificing nature. How can a physical body abuse another physical body? That is inert and this also is inert. How can inert things criticize or admonish? They cannot. How can they even worship any-thing? They cannot. But then can *Atma* criticize another *Atma?* That is absurd.

8

GOD EXISTS

One person who has seen God, says *"God exists"*. Another person who has not seen God says, *'God does not exist"* If a person has not seen God, then how can he assert that God does not exist? Here, for example, is *Nanjundaiah*. The one who sees *Nanjundaiah* declares that this is *Nanjundaiah*. If you point out *Chakravarti* to one who knows *Nanjundaiah*, saying "This *is Nanjundaiah"* the answer will be*" No, he is not Nanjundaiah"*. A person who has never seen *Nanjundaiah,* cannot say whether *Nanjundaiah* is here or not. Only one who has seen another person is able to declare whether that person is here or not. In the same way, only that person who has seen *God* and knows *God,* has the authority to declare that God exists. One may assert and the other may negate, but the object itself remains all the same. For both, God exists, because all there is, is only this one *Atma*, this one *Brahman*. *Brahman* is *Atma,* and beyond that nothing else exists.

WHAT IS THE MEANING OF DEVOTION?

Many people aspire for Grace, Love, Devotion and Humility. All these are forms of the *Atma*. God is not different from Faith. Faith and God are One and the same. Love Is God. Devotion is God. They are not different entities. What is the meaning of Devotion?

Devotion is that which enables the unmanifested Divine Principle to manifest itself in the *Inner Vision* of the devotee. Then for that devotee, nothing else will exist other than 'He'. To reach that stage you must discharge your duties keeping the *Permanent Entity* constantly in mind.

You can cross the vast deep ocean of worldly existence, and enjoy the infinite divinity that is its reality, with the help of a small boat. That boat is the name of God. In the beginning of a spiritual journey, the *Divine Name* is the basis for progress, but it should not become a life-long support, depending entirely on it alone.

Whatever service you are rendering, you should not feel that you are serving others, but that you are serving God himself. While taking a bath or giving one to the children, consider that you are doing the purification ritual of washing God himself. While serving food, consider that you are offering it to God himself. While giving food to a beggar, consider that God has come in this form, and you are serving Him. It seems that it is a beggar who is asking, but it is the *Atma* which is really enjoying the food you give. When you are cutting some vegetables for cooking, consider that you are cutting away your desires and ego with the knife of wisdom. While sweeping the floors at home, don't lament, "*Oh, it keeps getting dirty again and again*". Think rather that you are cleaning your own heart. If you are rolling chappati's at home, consider what joy it is to roll and knead and expand your heart. In this way, you can consider every activity that you undertake as being done for the sake of God. Then, where is the need for any separate meditation, separate penance, or separate worship?

THE ONLY SPIRITUAL EXERCISE
YOU NEED TO PERFORM

Consider your heart as *Atma*. Soften it and make it full of compassion. That is the only spiritual practice you need to perform. *Narasimhan* has told you that so many people are coming to *Prasanthi Nilayam* from different parts of the world. What brings them here? Are invitations sent? Does anyone ask them to come? It is only on account of the Love that is here and felt heart to heart. Through Love you can accomplish anything in the world.

Consider Love as the *Atma* itself. However, many scriptures you may read, and however many spiritual exercises you may do, if you do not allow your heart to melt with compassion, your life will be a sheer waste. All practices must be directed towards softening your heart, so that it will flow with kindness and *love*. Develop this feeling of compassion and allow it to flow fully and spread among all the people of the world.

Bhagavan Sri Sathya Sai Baba's Discourse in
Prasanthi Nilayam Mandir 30-03-87

2

YOU AND THE COSMOS

How can *Sai* be pleased with you.
If your thoughts are not good,
if your words are not pleasing,
if your actions are not right?
Good thoughts, sweet speech
and right conduct, these alone
Constitute true education.

To lead a purposeful and worthy life, you must recognize the true meaning of the body, the senses, the mind and the intellect and know how to use them intelligently and effectively. All the troubles of mankind are because 99% of people lead lives without understanding this truth.

The body, the senses, the mind, and the intellect, are only instruments for the individual and have no *Chaitanya* (*Consciousness*) of their own. The body is inert. Beginning as a mere mass of flesh, it grows into a handsome boy. Man imagines that the body has consciousness and is not an inert mass, but it is not the body that is the cause of this growth and change.

To cite an example, if you sweep your house every day and throw the dust into a dustbin, in due course there will be a big dust heap. Can consciousness be attributed to the dust heap because of its growth over a period? Likewise, the body grows on account of the food consumed by it. See what happens to the body when food is denied for some days. It ceases to grow; in fact, it begins to deteriorate. The body is only a temporary rest-house for the spirit.

Vedanta declares '*The body is a shrine for the Eternal Spirit inhabiting it*'. It is necessary, in this context, to know what enables the body, the senses, the mind, and the intellect, to develop or to deteriorate? The whole *Cosmos* is made up of the *Five Basic Elements, Pancha Bhootas: (Space, Air, Fire, Water, and Earth)*. Their subtle qualities are represented by *Sound, Touch, Form, Taste, and Smell*. All these have emerged from *Sat-Chit-Ananda (Being – Awareness – Bliss)*, the Primal Source.

THE FIVE ELEMENTS

Akasha (Space or Ether) provides the initial impulse. It is comparable to an infinite container. The other four elements *Air, Fire, Water and Earth* are contained in it. These elements vary in their order of subtlety. Water is subtler than Earth and is more expansive and lighter than Earth. Fire is subtler than Water and Air is subtler than Fire and more pervasive. Akasha (Space or Ether) is subtler than Air and is all-pervasive. Each of these elements is covered by a sheath (*Kosa*). *The Mind, The Intellect, The Will, and The Ego,* are enveloped by these sheaths.

Akasha (Space or Ether) is activated by what is called *Athigathi (very high-speed motion or vibrations)*. These vibrations by their movement give rise to Air. The movement of Air results in Fire (or heat). It is a scientific fact that friction causes heat, as in the case of the rubbing of the palms. To generate heat, air is necessary. When the heat cools off, water is produced. fluids solidify into earth. Hence, the starting point for the five elements is the *Akasha* (Space). These elements have come into existence for sustaining the Universe and demonstrating the *Omnipresence* and *Omniscience* of God.

THE MIND AND THE BODY

In the human being, the *Antahkarana* (The Inner Instrument) is made up of the Mind, the Intellect, the Will, and the Ego. The Ego is linked to the Life Principle (*Prana*). It is encased in the *Vijnana Maya Kosa* (the sheath of integrated awareness). The *Mind* is linked to the Will (*Chitta*) and is encased in the *Manomana Kosa* (the mental sheath). Thus, between the individual soul and the vital principle (*Prana*), the mind functions. The life principle functions between the mind and the body. The intellect (*Buddhi*) functions above the level of the mind. Both the intellect and the vital principle (*Prana*) are surcharged with heat (*Agni*). It is their combined presence in the body that accounts for the heat in the body. The mind should not be treated as something trivial. Man comprehends the world through the mind and hence its working should be completely watched. Because the mind is located between the intellect (*Buddhi*) and the *Prana* (the vital principle) both of which are filled with the fire principle-it tends to melt. The presiding Deity for the mind is the Moon. The Moon represents coolness and fluidity. Fluids like water, tend to flow down and find their level. Fire, on the contrary, has the tendency to go up. The mind, because of its watery nature, has the tendency to move downwards to get interested in petty things. Efforts must be made to make the mind look upwards.

THE PRIMAL SOURCE
THE FIVE ELEMENTS AND MAN

It should be remembered that the *Mind, the Intellect, the Will, and the Ego,* are made up of the Five Elements, which are all emanations from the *Supreme* – the *Sat-Chit-Ananda* (*Being – Awareness – Bliss*). This is their primal source from which they have emanated like innumerable sparks from a fire. From this source, they emerge as billions of atoms and assume countless forms. Man should realize that he has also come from the same Divine Source.

Endowed with the human form and gifted with sense organs, the mind, and the will, man nevertheless is failing to remember the Source from which he came. What is the cause for the body? The root cause is ignorance. Ignorance robs man of the power of discrimination. Lacking this capacity, man tends to inflate his Ego (*Ahamkaram*). Egoism breeds hatred which is the cause of attachment and desires. All actions (*Karmas*) are born of attachment and desires. Hence, the primary cause of birth in a human body is one's *Karma.*

THE COSMIC DELUSION

What is the ignorance which afflicts Man? It is the false vision that mistakes the Un-Real for the Real, and the Real for the Un-Real. An episode in the *Mahabharata* illustrates how this happens. Recognizing the supreme virtuousness of *Dharmaja,* the eldest of the *Pandavas, Maya,* the architect of the *Asuras,* offered to build a unique mansion for him in his capital at the time of the *Rajasooya Yajna* performed by *Dharmaja.*

This mansion, the *Maya Sabha* had one remarkable feature. Where there was no water, a pond would appear to exist. Where there was a pool, there would be no appearance of water. Where there was no door, a door would seem to exist, and a door would be present in an apparently blank wall. It was unique in producing illusions of this kind. *Duryodhana, Dussasana,* and other *Kauravas,* came to see this mansion. Imagining that there was water in one place, they lifted their clothes only to find that there was no water at all. At another place, they drenched themselves, because they stridently walked into a pool, not seeing the water in it.

What is the inner meaning of this story of the *Maya Sabha?* The cosmos itself is one vast *Maya Sabha* (a mansion of delusions). Attachment and hatred are represented by *Duryodhana, and Dussasana. Dussasana* means one who is a violator of the rule of law. *Duryodhana,* is one who misuses his strength and abilities.

In every Man, there are these traits of *Duryodhana,* and *Dussasana.* In life, everyone has to adhere to certain regulations. In the *Sathya Sai* institute, for instance, there are regulations relating to the conduct of students in the hostel and elsewhere. It is only when these regulations are observed strictly that they can call themselves 'Seekers of Knowledge" (*Vidyarti's*). When students misuse their talents and skills, they become weak and go astray.

MISUSE OF SENSES

How does this misuse take place? The eyes are misused by looking at undesirable objects. The tongue is misused by indulging in evil talk. The ears, the heart, and the hands, are all misused in different ways. Misuse occurs whenever a Divinely endowed capacity or talent is used for wrongful purposes. It is misdirection of energy. If students indulge in such misuse, they turn into *Duryodhana's,* and *Dussasanas,* and come to grief like them. Hence, no one should misuse any of the powers with which he is endowed. It amounts to an affront to God who is the Source of all powers.

Everyone thinks that it is his sense organs – his eyes, ears, etc. – that enable him to experience and comprehend the world. How true is this? In the dream state none of the senses are functioning. And yet, one has the experience of seeing, talking, hearing, walking, and doing other actions. What is the eye that sees in the dream? What is the tongue that talks? In the dream state, the mind does all the functions of the sense organs which are dormant at the time. When you feel in a dream that you are walking in a forest, it is not your legs that are walking. It is the mind which does the walking. It is the mind that assumes all the functions of the senses. The entire world is a projection of the mind. When the mind is properly directed, all the senses will be under control. When you water the roots of a tree, all the branches and leaves will get the benefit.

MENTAL ABERRATIONS

The mind is subject to fancies and aberrations. In poor light, you mistake a rope for a snake and are filled with fear. When light is brought, you find there is no snake. The appearance and disappearance of fear are mental aberrations. The rope was there all the time. The idea of a snake was superimposed on it by the fancies of the mind.

HOW IS ONE TO GET RID OF THE DELUSION?

Brahman (God) cannot be experienced unless one gets rid of the delusions of the mind. How is one to get rid of the delusions; by developing faith in the Omnipresence of God. This faith can grow when one realizes that every object in the world needs a basis for its existence and support. God is the basis and support for the entire Cosmos. The *Vedas* are the authority for accepting God as the Source of everything in Creation. If one can accept the authority of the ordinary almanac for recognizing a particular date in the calendar, why should one refuse to accept the authority of the *Vedas* regarding the nature of the *Atma* and the *Brahman.* There is authority in the *Vedas* for everything we experience in daily life. The *Vedas* have recognized the uniqueness of human birth and proclaimed the existence of God. It is illogical for man to accept his uniqueness as a human being on the authority of the scriptures, and at the same time deny the existence of God.

NATURE AND DIVINITY

How misconceptions and doubts can arise may be seen from a scientific example. When you hold a mirror before you, your image is reflected by the mirror, but the image is not in the mirror. The reflection is seen because of the mercury coated surface at the back of the mirror. Seeing the image, you imagine that it is in the mirror. You imagine also that it is a true reflection of yourself. This also is not true. In the image, your right eye appears as your left eye and the left eye as the right eye. Hence the image is not a true reflection of yourself. Likewise, Nature is a vast mirror. You regard as real the varied objects you see in Nature, but they are all different forms of God. The One willed to become the many. This truth is recognized by all religions. Man forgets this truth and leads a life divorced from faith in God.

ACTIONS AND RESULTS

Students! You may yourself enquire into the basis for this creation. To start with, you try to find out what causes dreams.

Some may say 'thoughts' are the cause. Some others may attribute dreams to 'the kind of food that is consumed'. Neither of these is correct. The fact is, that it is sleep that is the cause of dreams. Where there is no sleep, there are no dreams. So, to the questions, "What is the cause of creation?" the answer is *Ignorance* (*Ajnana*). For example: During the summer, the land gets heated up and is completely barren. As soon as there is rainfall, things begin to sprout, and the land looks green. From where did the sprout come? Before sprouting, the seeds remained in the earth and when the rains came, they began to sprout. If there had been no seeds earlier, the sprouting would not have occurred.

Likewise, *Karma* (past deeds), is the seed for human birth. Your present life is a reaction, resound, and reflection of your past actions. Therefore, you are advised to: "*Be Good, See Good, and Do Good*". When you perform any actions, you do not think about the long-term consequences. You are preoccupied with the concerns of the moment, but when the final results come, you are frightened. Whether the results are pleasant or unpleasant, they are inescapable. If sugar is dissolved in water, even if you think it is poison, it will only do you good. But, if poison is put in the water and you drink it, thinking it is sugar cane juice, it will be fatal. If you regard something bad as good and act on it, the results are bound to be bad.

It is his conduct that is most important for every person. Conduct is determined by the state of the mind. Instead of giving way to the mind, the results are based on your actions and not on your fancies. In promptings of the senses, every action should be done as a sacred offering to God. You should be indifferent to censure or praise. Such equanimity can only come from faith in God. Lacking this faith and filled with the conceit that he is 'the Doer' of everything, man gets immersed in trouble and sorrow. The one who boasts about his achievements should recognize equally, that he is the author of his misfortunes. He cannot claim to be the 'Doer' and at the same time deny responsibility for the consequences of his actions.

DO YOUR DUTY AND LEAVE
THE RESULTS TO GOD

Hence, in all your actions, whether good or bad, do your duty, leaving the results to God. The flowers that you may offer in your *Puja*, will not please *Sai*. It is what you offer from the lotus of your heart that will please *Sai*. Consider everything in nature as gifts of *God*. When you offer anything, have the sacred feeling that you are offering to God what he has given to you. When you feel and act in this way, your life will be filled with peace and joy. Have the firm conviction that the Cosmos and God are not different. Look upon creation as the manifestation of God and make proper use of your opportunities to experience God.

In your studies, try to combine spiritual discipline with academic pursuits. Only then will you find fulfilment in education. Every one of you should become an ideal person. You must develop the habit of examining yourself and correcting yourself. Self-correction and Self-punishment are as important as Self-realization. Your senses, like the eyes, the ears, and the tongue, are God given gifts. They should be used only for sacred purposes and should not be misused. There is only one royal road to realizing God. It is the path of Divine Love.

You have come from God and your destiny is to merge in God. Entertain only sacred thoughts and engage yourselves only in sacred deeds. Thereby, you will be sanctifying your lives.

(Excerpt taken from Bhagavan's Discourse at the Sri Sathya Sai Institute, Students Hostel, Vidyagiri October 2nd, 1988)

3

GOD AND MAN
NARAYANA AND NARA

'*Everything in its own good time*', they say; the fruit must grow and ripen before the sourness is turned to sweetness. I have been coming to this town for ten years, but it is only this evening that you, in this vast multitudinous gathering, have been able to derive this bliss of hearing Me discoursing! I am happy to meet all of you in one auspicious hour, all collected in one place. All that I can tell you about the spiritual discipline has been told often before. Man's capacity, his nature, his talents, are all ancient possessions, and so the advice regarding how to use them is also very ancient.

The only new thing is man's perverse behavior – the directions in which he has been wasting his talents, misusing his capacity and playing false to his own nature. He has been forgetting the path prescribed in the scriptures, for the cultivation of his nature, hence all this suffering, and hence also My Advent.

Man is essentially a discriminating animal, endowed with *Viveka*. He is not content with the satisfaction of mere animal needs. He feels some void, some deep discontent, some unslaked thirst, for he is a child of immortality, and he feels that death is not, and should not be the end. This *Viveka* urges man to discover answers to the problems that haunt him: *"Where did I come from, where am I journeying, which, is the journeys end?"* So, *Buddhi* (the intellect) has to be kept sharp and clear.

There are three types of *Buddhi* according to the dominance of one or other of the three *Gunas*: *Thamas*, (inertia or sloth) which sees *Sathyam* (truth) as *Asathyam* (untruth), and sees *Asathyam* as *Sathyam*; *Rajas* (passion or activity) which like a pendulum swings from one to the other, hovering between the two, unable to distinguish between them; and *Sathwa*, (purity or serenity) which knows which is *Sathyam,* and which is *Asathyam.*

MY ADVENT

The world today is suffering from passionate intellect (*Rajo-buddhi*); the attachment to superficial appearances, rather than inertia intellect (*Thamo-buddhi*). People have violent likes and dislikes; they have become fanatical and factious. They are carried away by pomp and noise, show and propaganda; that is why discrimination has become necessary. To reach the goal, *Sathwa Buddhi* (equanimous intellect) is essential. It will seek the truth calmly and stick with it whatever the consequences.

I have come to help all to acquire this *Sathwic* (serene nature). You might have heard people talk about the miracles; of My '*materializing this*' and '*giving that*', of My fulfilling all your wants, of My curing your illnesses, but they are not so important as the *Satwaguna* (poised equanimous state), I appreciate, promote and instill. Of course, I confer on you these boons of health and prosperity, but only so that you might, with greater enthusiasm and with less interruption, proceed with spiritual *Sadhana*.

Eat well, so that your physical faculties might grow, and the good physique will in turn develop your intelligence more fully. *Bhakti* (devotion) leads to *Sakthi* (power), and *Sakthi* will grant *Yukthi* (skill). The *Yukthi* will help you to fix your *Rakthi* (attachment), on the proper objects and your *Bhakti,* thus promoted, finally results in *Mukthi* (Liberation).

Pay special attention to the healthcare of the body, to escape the overpowering handicaps of poverty; but you must ever be cautious that you are not caught in the trap of forgetting the transience of all this. Bring your thoughts constantly back to the Eternal *Soul (Atma)*, which is the source of the objective world and the basic reality behind all these appearances.

ATMA-VICHARA – SELF-ENQUIRY

The first step in Atma-Vichara (enquiring about the Self) is the practice of the truth that '*whatever gives you pain, gives pain to others, and whatever gives you joy, gives joy to others.*' So, do unto others as you would like them to do unto you. Desist from any act in relation to others, which if done by them would give you pain. Thus, a kind of reciprocal relationship will grow between you and others, to gradually reach the stage when your heart thrills with joy if others are joyful, and shudders in pain when others are sad. This is not the kind of affection towards those who are dear to you, or those who are your kith and kin. That is a sign of delusion; but this sharing of joy and grief is automatic, immediate, and universal. It is a sign of great spiritual advance. Then, the wave knows that it is part of the ocean, and that all waves are but temporary manifestations of the self-same sea having a taste of the ocean itself.

The others are part of yourself; you need not worry about them; worry about yourself, that is enough. When you become all right, they too will become all right, for you will no longer be aware of them as separate from you. Criticizing others, finding fault with them, all comes out of egoism. Search for your own faults instead; the faults you see in others are but reflections of your own personality traits. Pay no heed to little worries; attach your mind to the Lord. Then you will be led on to the company of good men and your talents will be transmuted.

IF YOU WANT TO ATTAIN ME – CULTIVATE LOVE

Be like a bee drinking the nectar of every flower, not the mosquito drinking blood and distributing disease in return. First, consider all as children of the Lord, as your own brothers and sisters. Develop the quality of Love. Always seek the welfare of humanity. Love, and you will be loved in return. Hate will never be your lot if you promote love and look upon all with love. That is the one lesson I teach always; that is My secret too. If you want to attain me, cultivate love, give up hatred, envy, anger, cynicism, and falsehood. I do not ask that you should be a scholar or a recluse, or an ascetic skilled in *Japa,* and *Dhyana,* (recitation of the holy name) *and* (meditation). Is your heart full of love? That is all I examine!

Believe that Love is God, Truth is God, Love is Truth, Truth is Love; for it is only when you love that you have no fear, for fear is the mother of falsehood. If you have no fear, you will adhere to truth. The mirror of *Prema* (love) reflects the *Atma* in you, and reveals to you that the *Atma* is Universal, Immanent in every being.

24

CULTIVATE VINAYA – HUMILITY

I shall not tell you very complex matters. I shall give only simple remedies for the ills you are suffering from. I find here a large number of students. Well, what are they studying for? What is the goal? How are we to judge that they have studied well, by the salary that they are able to get, or the position they are able to secure? No. Education must result in the development of *Viveka* (discrimination) and *Vinaya* (humility). The educated man must be able to discriminate between the momentary and the momentous, the lasting and the effervescent. He must not run after glitter and glamour, but he must seek instead the good and the golden. He must know how to keep the body in good trim, the senses under strict control, the mind well within check, the intellect sharp and clear, unhampered by prejudices and hatreds, and the feelings untouched by egoism. He must know the soul (*Atma*) too, for that is his very core; that is the effulgence which illumines his inner and outer selves. This knowledge will ensure joy, peace, and courage for him throughout his life. Students must also cultivate *Vinaya*; the art of avoiding inflicting pain on others.

BE GRATEFUL TO YOUR PARENTS

I must also tell the students that they must be grateful to the parents who give them all the facilities they now enjoy, at great sacrifice. In fact, the parents must be worshipped as visible representations of the Godhead; they are responsible for your very existence, and for all this joy and adventure in the physical and spiritual spheres. For this reason, they must be tended, respected and worshipped.

"Mother! Mother! Look, I've brought a little food for you"
Listen a little to this story. *'Once there was a boy who was begging in the streets for food, so that he could keep his*

bedridden mother and two little sisters alive. One night, when he clamoured in front of a rich man's house, the master got enraged at his piteous cries. The boy was very unlucky that day as he had collected only a few morsels, and the hour was nearing nine. So, he cried most pathetically, and it aroused the anger of the rich man inside the mansion. He came out and kicked the boy into the gutter. He was already very weak for he was starving to feed his mother and sisters. So, when he fell, he breathed his last, wailing "Mum! Here is a little food for you" His hand held the bowl firm, even when it had become lifeless!'

Such is the devotion that the mother invokes, and which she deserves, for all the pain she endured and all the sacrifice she bore in order that the son might be healthy, happy and good. Show that gratitude, boys, to the parents. Remember them and pay them the tribute of at least a tear on the anniversary of their passing away. Do it with *Shraddha* (faith). That is why it is called *Shraddha*, not that the offerings you make reach them or that they are waiting for them in some other world. It is a tribute that you should offer in gratitude for the great chance they gave you for this sojourn in the world, with all the wonderful opportunities it offers for Self-Realization.

PARENTS ARE SERVANTS
APPOINTED BY THE LORD

Parents too must encourage children when they evince any interest in spiritual advance and study. They must also set them good examples. Among the children that are before Me here, there may be a *Vivekananda* and many a *Thyagaraja.* Children must be given every facility to develop the divine talents that are in them. Parents must feel that they are servants appointed by the Lord to tend the little souls that are born in their households, as the gardener tends the trees in the garden of the master. They must arouse the latent goodness in these tiny hearts, by telling stories about the saints and sages of the past. They must see that children do not develop fear and become cowards afraid of walking straight.

YOU ARE ALL THE INDESTRUCTIBLE ATMA-BELIEVE ME

You are all the indestructible *Atma* (soul), believe me, nothing need discourage you. In dreams you suffer so much; loss of money, fire, food, insult etc., but you are not affected at all. When these things happen during the waking stage, you feel afflicted. Really, it is not the real you, that suffers all that. Give up the delusion that you are this physical entity, and you become really free.

DEVELOP TRUTH AND LOVE

Lastly, about Myself, no one can understand My Mystery. The best you can do is to get immersed in it. It is no use arguing about pros and cons. If you want to know the depths of the ocean, dive in! If you want to know the taste of a dish, eat it! Only then can you discuss Me to your hearts content.

Develop *Sathya* (truth) *and Prema* (love) and then you need not even pray to Me to grant you this and that. Everything will be added unto you, unasked. *Nara* (man) *and Narayana* (God) are the two wires, the positive and the negative, which combine to bring electricity through. *Nara* co-operates with *Narayana,* and becomes the vehicle of Divine power, when he acquires the two qualities, *Sathya and Prema* (truth and love).

Bhagavan Sri Sathya Sai Baba's Discourse
in Nellore July 25th, 1958

27

4

I WANT YOU TO BE ACTIVE

I have come to comfort your life, not to describe mine, so I do not like *Ramanatha Reddy* and *Kasturi* speaking about Me and the incidents of My Life! Your lives are more important for me, for My Purpose is to see that you live more happily and with greater contentment. All beings have to do *Karma* (sanctified activity). It is a universal, inescapable obligation. Some feel that only *Punya* and *Papa*, meritorious and sinful, virtuous or vicious deeds, are entitled to be called *Karma,* but your very breathing is *Karma.* There are certain *Karma's*, the fruits of which you cannot give up. There are physical, mental and spiritual *Karma's* and doing each one of these for your own spiritual elevation is an offering to God.

Mention was made of *Puttaparthi*, and you were advised to go there and draw inspiration from *bhajan's* there. Please do not incur the expense; for wherever you are and whenever you call on Me, your room can become *Prasanthi Nilayam*, your village can be made *Puttaparthi*. I am ever ready to respond, ever ready to listen and reply to your prayers.

I want you to be active, fully engaged, for if you have no activities, time will hang heavily on your hands. Do not waste a single moment of the allotted span of life, for time is the body of God. He is known as *Kalaswarupa,* (the form of time). It is a crime to misuse time, or to waste it in idleness. So too, the physical and mental talents given to you by the Lord as capital for the business of living, should not be frittered away. Like the force of gravitation which drags everything down, the *Thamo-sakthi,* or (the *pull of sloth*), will drag you relentlessly down, so you must be ever on the watch, be ever active.

Like the brass vessel which must be scrubbed to a nice shine, the mind of man has also to be scrubbed, by means of *Sadhana* (spiritual discipline): that is to say, activity like *Japam,* (repetition of God's name) *and Dhyana* (meditation)*. Karma,* which is natural, and like breathing, automatically becomes *Vikarma* (an impious act) when it is done consciously, with a definite result in view.

A HINDU AND HIS ENGLISH FRIEND

A Hindu and his English friend once happened to come to the banks of the Godavari River. The Hindu said, *"I will bathe in this sacred water"*. He recited the Name of *Hari* (God) as he plunged in and came out refreshed in mind as well as body. He felt great happiness that he got the rare chance of a bath in the holy river. The English man laughed and said," *This is mere H2O. How can you get unspeakable joy by dipping into it? It is all superstition"* But the Hindu replied, *"Leave me to my superstition-you can stick with your superstition"*

The cynic got only physical cleanliness, but the believer got mental purity also.

VIKARMAS

When you prostrate before the elders, the mind too must be humble. It is not the body alone that should bend. Now there are many social workers in Madras who visit hospitals and do service to the patients there. Most of the work they do is mechanical, like fanning the patients, writing letters for them, and singing *bhajans*, without paying heed to the actual requirements of the patients. Many do this work because it is the current mode of social service, but it must be *Karma*, done with the full co-operation of the mind, gladly, intelligently, reverentially. The patient should not feel disgusted at the fussiness of the social worker. He should be looking forward to the arrival of that person, of someone who is very near and dear. If you do not like that type of work, you need not engage yourselves in it. Do not burden your mind by the unpleasantness of the task. Work done mechanically is like the flame of an oil-less wick. The oil is mental enthusiasm; pour it and the lamp will burn clear and long.

WHEN ACTIONS BECOME SACRED

In fact, *Karma* becomes *Yoga* when it is done without any attachment. A *Sannyasi* (monk) should not even remember whatever he does. He should not do any *Karma* anticipating any result. That is the *Nishkama* (desireless) ideal at its highest. The best *Karma* is that which is done at the call of duty, because it must be done, not because it is advantageous to do so. The *Sannyasi* should have no anger, anxiety, envy, or greed, but your experience must be telling you that *Sannyasi's* who are free from these are very rare today. Do not even cast your glance at a *Sannyasi* who is so false to his vow that he craves for name and fame or indulges in calumny or competition. Do not be led away by such persons into disbelieving the S*astras* and the *Vedas*. He who is firmly fixed in the faith that this world is a mirage of the mind, he alone is *Swami*. The others are mere *Ramaswamy's,* or *Krishnaswamy's,* entitled to have the epithet *Swami* at the end of the name, not at the beginning.

REPEAT THE NAME OF THE LORD

Prakriti (nature) is a very ancient entity. It is *Purathana*. The *Jeevi* too is *Purathana* having had many previous entries and exits, but now it has come in with a new dress. It is *Nuthana* (modern), coming like a pilgrim to a holy place for going the rounds. The *Jeevi* must have a guide who will show the spots and help fulfil the pilgrimage. That guide is the Lord himself. The guidebooks are the *Vedas*, the *Upanishads*, and the *Shastras* (*spiritual texts*). The essence of the scriptures lies in this one rule: Repeat the Name of the Lord, and always guard His Glory in your Spirit.

THE LORD IS AS THE KALPATHARU –
THE DIVINE WISH FULFILLING TREE

The Lord is as the *Kalpatharu,* the Divine Wish-Fulfilling Tree that gives whatever is asked, but you must go near the tree and wish for the thing that you want. The *atheist* is the person who keeps far from the tree, the *theist* is the one who has come near; that is the difference. The tree does not make any distinction. It grants boons to all. The Lord will not punish, or take revenge if you do not recognize Him, or revere Him. He has no special type of worship which alone can please Him.

OM IS THE SYMBOL OF THE OMNIPRESENT GOD

If you have the ear, you can hear '*Om*' announcing the Lord's presence in every sound. All the five elements produce this sound, '*Om*'. The bell in the temple is intended to convey the '*Om*' as the symbol of the Omnipresent God. When the bell sounds '*Om*' the Godhead within you will awaken, and you will be aware of His Presence. That is the meaning of the bell which is rung in the front of the inner shrine in the temple.

APPROACH GOD WITHOUT FEAR

Earn the right to approach the Lord without fear, and the right to ask for your heritage. You must become so free, that praise will not emanate from you when you approach the Lord. Praise is a sign of distance and fear. You must have heard the Kalidasa story. "*He said that he would get liberation as soon as 'I go' – that is to say, as soon as the ego disappears, for then he shines in his native splendor, as Brahman, or as the indestructible Atma. The 'I' when crossed out becomes the symbol of the cross; so, what is crucified is the ego, remember then, that the Divine Nature manifests itself unhampered!*"

DO YOUR SPIRITUAL DISCIPLINE IN AN
ATMOSPHERE OF JOY

The ego is most easily destroyed by devotion (*Bhakthi*), by dwelling on the Magnificence of the Lord and by rendering service to others, as children of the Lord. You can call on the Lord by any name, for all names are his. Select the name and the form that appeals to you most. That is why *Sahasranamas* are composed for the various forms of God. You have the freedom and the right to select any one of the thousand. The *Guru* will give you the name and the form suited to your temperament and *Samskaras* (meritorious acts). If the *Guru* commands under a threat and orders you to adopt a *Sadhana* declaring "This is my *Ajna* (command)" then you can tell him that the main thing is your satisfaction, not his. You must do the *Sadhana* in an atmosphere of joy and contentment.

The *Guru* should not force the disciple to grow with a bent in the direction that he prefers. The disciple has the right to develop on his own lines according to his *Samskaras* and bent of mind. The old relationship of *Guru* and *Shishya's* (disciple) has today become topsy-turvy.

Rich and influential *shishya's* now rule the *Guru* and dictate how he should behave, and the *Guru* also, keen on accumulating fame and wealth, stoops to the tactics recommended by the *Shishya's,* and thus lowers his status. So, examine the *Guru* and his credentials, his ideals and practice before accepting him. Even in My case, do not be distracted by stories of what I 'create' by a wave of the hand. Do not jump to conclusions with closed eyes. Watch, study, and weigh. Never yield to anyone, unless you feel the inner satisfaction that you are on the right path. Above all, do not speak ill of great men and sages. That is the sign of growing egoism and the childish impertinence born of that conceit.

MY ADVICE TO YOU

My advice to you today is this. Just as you attend to the needs of the body, feeding it three times a day, to keep it in good running condition, so too, spend some time regularly every day to keep your inner consciousness also in good trim. Spend one hour in the morning, another at night and a third in the early hours of dawn, the *Brahma-Muhurta*, as it is called, for *Japam* and meditation on the Lord. You will find great peace descending on you, and great new sources of strength welling up within you as you progress in this *Sadhana*. After some time, the mind will dwell on the name wherever you are, and whatever you are engaged in, and then peace and joy will be your inseparable companions.

Bhagavan Sri Sathya Sai Discourse,
Gokkale hall, Madras March 25th, 1958

5

THE DIVINE POWER IN MAN

sssssssssssssssssssssssssssssssssssssssssssssssssssssssss
Oh Man! If The Divine Lord Is Not Visible to You,
Just as The Stars Cannot Be Seen in Daylight,
Because You Are Blinded by Ignorance,
Do Not Deny His Existence.
sssssssssssssssssssssssssssssssssssssssssssssssssssssss

EMBODIMENTS OF DIVINE LOVE

From the most ancient times, man has been engaged in the search
for God. The questions, "Who is God?" and "What is the means
to realize God?" are not of today. They have been there from
the earliest times and have agitated mankind ceaselessly. A few
*Yogi*s who comprehended the nature of God, and who felt that
the purpose of human existence is to seek God, undertook various spiritual exercises to discover how to achieve this objective.

THE SOUL PURPOSE OF HUMAN LIFE

The purpose of human life is to realize God. It is in this context that human birth becomes the rarest among all living beings. The ancient Sages, recognizing this truth, pursued different kinds of penances to experience God. Some of them, feeling that the task was beyond their powers, gave up the quest in the middle. Some others, recognizing that this was the sole purpose of human life, persevered in their efforts with determination.

When man sets his heart upon achieving anything, there is nothing impossible for him. But, immersed in worldly pleasures, man becomes a prey to weakness and forgets his divine nature. Few care to enquire into the real value of these mundane pleasures, or their ephemeral nature.

What is the difference between man and bird and beast? Can eating, drinking, sleeping and ultimately dying, be the Be-All-and-End-All of human life? All these are common to animals and human beings. What then, is the difference? Although man is endowed with intelligence, discrimination, and wisdom, without endeavoring to know the truth, man regards physical phenomena as the only reality, God as remote from him, and thus, forgets the main goal of life.

THE EXPERIENCE OF THE SAGES

The ancient Sages however, regarded realization of God as their main goal and practiced various austerities. Thereafter, they went out into the world and proclaimed: "Oh Man! We have experienced the effulgent, all pervading supreme Divine" (*Vedaham Etham Purusham Mahantham*)" Where did they experience him? They declared: "*We have found Him, beyond the darkness, beyond the mind and the senses, in our hearts*"

Man is a combination of the body, the mind, and the Spirit

(*Atma*). He is thus the embodiment of these three, but forgetting the mind and the *Atma*, when man identifies himself solely with the body, he reduces himself to an animal. When he forgets the *Atma* and the body, and identifies himself with the mind alone, he becomes a demon (*Danava*). When one forgets the body and the mind, one becomes God.

BODY-MIND AND SPIRIT

The body is the instrument of action. The mind is the instrument of cognition. The *Atma* is steady and unwavering. Corresponding to these three are *Karma* (action), *Upasana* (ritual worship) and *Bhakti* (devotion). What is the difference between *Bhakti* and *Upasana?* In both, *Prema* (love of God) is inherent. *Bhakti* and *Prema* are synonymous. Contemplating on God, forgetting the world, living in a state of *Bliss* (ananda) is *Prapathi* (total surrender to God).

DURGA, LAKSHMI, AND SARASWATHI

Bhartiya's have been celebrating the *Navarathri* Festival from ancient times as a mode of worship of *Devi* (The divine as mother). They worship *Durga, Lakshmi, and Saraswathi* during these nine days. Who are these three? They are three forms which have fascinated *Brahminchina* (man). Their esoteric significance is represented by three *Sakthi's* (potencies). They are *Karma, Upasana,* and *Jnana.* These potencies have been given other names.

The concept of total surrender (*Prapathi*) is related to Self-Realization (Oneness with God). God, in fact, dwells in every human being as the *Atma.* The body is the sacred abode of the *Atma.* Hence the scriptures declare: *'The Body is the Temple of God in which the individual Spirit dwells as the ancient One."*

37

Just as the diamond is found in clay and not in a rock, the spirit (as consciousness) resides in the earthly body. The body comes from the earth. The *Atma* is consciousness. Humanness is the coming together of the mundane and the spiritual consciousness. It is a combination of good and evil. It is a mixture of the transient and the eternal. Hence, for what *is Subha* (auspicious), or *Asubha* (inauspicious), for *Truth* (sathya), or *Asathya* (falsehood), *for Kshaya* (the perishable), *and Akshaya* (the imperishable), *the* prefix 'A' accounts for the difference. For instance, *Asathya* (untruth) is that which is not true (*Sathya*). The transient (*Anithya*) is that which is not permanent (*Nithya*). By understanding these distinctions, men have sought to realize God.

MISUSE OF THE BODY

The human body is precious. Man today, is not realizing what he owes to his body. The body, composed of the five elements, which has been given to man to understand his true nature; to recognize the truth about his immortal spirit, and to experience the eternal within him, is being used for the enjoyment of physical pleasures. The body surely has not been given for this purpose. The body is a shrine (*Kshetra*). The Indweller is the knower (*Kshetragna*). The relationship is that of body (*Sarira*) and the indweller (*Sariri*). Instead of recognizing this integral relationship, man is only concerned with the body and seeks to realize God. How is this possible? The first pre-requisite is for man to acquire the firm conviction, that God dwells in his heart.

THE INDWELLING GOD

There is no need to search for God elsewhere. There is no need to go to a forest and lead an austere life to experience God who is within each one. When man turns his vision inwardly, he can experience eternal bliss. The source of bliss, the spirit, is within himself. God is nearer to everyone than one's parents, spouse, or children. Kith and kin are outside oneself, but God is within the body. Forgetting God, who is nearest and closest to them, people are seeking an invisible God elsewhere. God appears in human form (*Daivam Manusharupena*). It is sheer human fancy to imagine that God is effulgent light, or that He has four arms, with conch and discus, and dwells in some remote place.

A man who is attached to the body can never experience a formless incorporeal God. Only when he gets rid of the body consciousness can he recognize the transcendental Divine. Hence, if one has attachment to the body, one must adore God in a physical form. It is a waste of time to try to secure one way or other a direct vision of God. God manifests Himself in the heart of everyone. The one supreme spirit is the indwelling spirit in all beings (*Ekatma Sarvabhutha – Antaratma*). The absolute reality (*Sath*) is One only, though the wise call it by many names. We must endeavor to experience that God in us.

THE THREE POTENCIES IN THE GAYATRI MANTRA

The significance of *Durga, Lakshmi,* and *Saraswathi* has to be rightly understood.

The three represent the three kinds of potencies in man.

Iccha Shakti: Will Power
Kriya Shakti: Power of Action and
Jnana Shakti: Power of Discrimination.

Saraswathi is manifest in man as the *Power of Speech* (*Vaak*), the power of words.

Durga is present in the form of Kriya Shakti: *the Power of Action* (dynamism).

Lakshmi is manifest in the form of man as *Will Power.*

The Body indicates *'Kriya Shakti'*

The Mind is the repository of *'Iccha Shakti'*

The *Atma* is *'Jnana Shakti'*

Kriya Sakti comes from the body, which is material.

The power that activates the body that is inert and makes it vibrant is *Iccha Sakti.*

The power that induces the vibrations of *Iccha Shakti* is *Jnana Sakti*, which causes radiation of energy. These three potencies are represented by the **Gayatri Mantra**:

'*Om Bhur-Bhuvah-Suvaha*', 'Bhu" represents *Bhu-Loka* (the Earth). '*Bhuvah*' represents the life force also meaning (the conscience in man), '*Suvaha*' represents the power of radiation. All the three are present in man, thus *Durga, Lakshmi,* and *Saraswathi* dwell in the human heart.

GAYATRI MANTRA

'Om Bhur Bhuvah Suvaha,
Tat Savitur Varenyam,
Bhargo Devasya Dhimahi,
Dhiyo Yo Nah Prachodayat'.

(This Original Image is of the Gayatri Maa
Temple in Prasanthi Nilayam)

41

SATHWAS, RAJAS, THAMAS

Men are prone to exhibiting *Rajasic* qualities like anger, and hatred. They are the menacing manifestations of *Durga*. The extolling of God in song and poetry, and the pleasing vibrations produced by them, indicates the power of *Saraswathi*. The pure qualities that arise in man such as compassion, love, forbearance, and sympathy are derived from *Lakshmi*.

When people worship *Durga, Lakshmi and Saraswathi* externally in pictures or icons, they are giving physical form to the subtle potencies that are within them. The unfortunate predicament of man today is that he is not recognizing the powers within him, nor developing respect for them. He goes after the external, attracted by the physical forms. The relationship between the material and the subtle must be understood.

The remedy for man's ills is contained within himself, but man seeks remedies from outside. Here is an illustration of what happens in the world: *A hotel and a drug store are adjacent to each other. When a hotel server gets a headache, he goes to the neighboring drug store for a pill to cure his headache. When the drug storekeeper gets a headache, he goes to the hotel for a cup of coffee to cure him, instead of taking one of his own pills.*

TURN YOUR VISION INWARDS

Likewise, people tend to ignore the divinity within them but hanker after many external objects. There is no need to go in search of God. Men must develop firm faith in the divinity within. They engage themselves in many outward spiritual practices (*sadhanas*) but these must be internalized. All scholarship is of no avail, if there is no realization in the heart. The scholar may expound the texts but lacks the internal experience. One who has mastered the *Vedas* may be able to explain the words, but cannot recognize the *Veda Purusha,* the supreme person hailed by the *Vedas.* When a person goes to a temple, he closes his eyes in front of the idol, because what he seeks is an internal vision of God and not a sight of the external form of the idol. God is Omnipresent, as proclaimed in the *Gita.* God Is One, though Names and Forms differ.

All education today is related to the physical world. It will not serve to reveal God. It was this which compelled *Shankaracharya* to teach a pundit who was learning by rote Panini's Grammar, that at the moment of death, only the Lord's Name *Govinda* will save him, and not the rules of grammar. Following this, Bhagavan sang several verses of the Bhajan. 'B*haja Govindam*' (a devotional song) of *Shankaracharya.*

PRACTICE AND PRECEPT

Though this teaching has been propagated for centuries, very few practice it. Many read the *Ramayana* as a daily ritual, but how many carry out the commands of their fathers? How many follow the practice of fraternal affection and love proclaimed in the *Ramayana*? Is there anyone standing for the gospel of *Dharma* (duty) as upheld by *Sri Rama*? Of what use it is to listen endlessly to discourses, without putting anything into practice? The *Gita* is being read and expounded all the time. Is a single precept from it being put into practice? Not at all! *The Gita* shows the path of God realization, but simply reciting the *Gita* is valueless. Follow the *Gita* and simply tread the path indicated by it. Only then will you reap the reward.

LOVE OF GOD

What is meant by practice? Direct your sacred love towards God. There is no need for any severe spiritual exercise. Love is God. Live in Love. Be always immersed in that Love. What should be pure love has been polluted today by all kinds of attachments. Pollution is all pervading and has spread to the hearts of people. Purity has become scarce. The Love of God (*Prema*) is all powerful. *Prahlada* demonstrated this all-conquering power of love for the Lord. He survived every kind of ordeal by his father through his faith in *Narayana* and his love for Him.

EMBODIMENTS OF LOVE!

Though people live in the phenomenal world and carry on their activities, they should perform all their actions as an offering to please the Lord.

What is it that you should do during the ten days of the *Navaratri Festival*?

1. Convert your *Iccha Sakti* (will power) into a yearning for God.
2. Convert *Kriya Sakti* (power of action) into a force for doing divine actions.
3. Convert your *Jnana Sakti* (power of discrimination) into God Itself.

'*Sathyam, Jnanam, Anantham Brahma*' God Is Truth, Wisdom, and Infinite) proclaim the scriptures.

These three are in man. You can experience the entire Cosmos within your heart. The marvelous powers in man, the power of sight, etc. are all derived from God. Human birth has to be redeemed by contemplation on God. Man today, is misusing his precious body. Instead of filling it with the nectar of love, he is filling it with worldly trash. Man should be the master of his senses, instead of being their slave.

Bhagavan concluded His discourse with the bhajan *'Prema Mudita Manase Kaho, Rama! Rama! Ram*, in the *Sai Ramesh Hall, Brindavan October 9th, 1994*

6

BELIEVE IN YOURSELF

I have been seeing your devotion and enthusiasm ever since I entered your town this morning, and during the procession through the streets, I could see the ardor of your *Bhakthi* (devotion). Even now, I feel that I could give you joy by merely sitting here and giving you *Darshan* (the vision of the Lord), for I can listen to your silent prayers, and you can sense My *Prema* (Divine Love). That is enough. That gives *Anandham*. You are born, you grow, you live, and you merge, all in *Anandham* (bliss). That is the truth, though very few know it. That is why I reminded you of it by addressing you as *Anandha-Swarupulara* (embodiments of bliss). Your *Swarupa* (natural state) is *Anandham* (bliss), however much you might have ignored it.

Bharath (India) has proclaimed this for ages. The *Vedas* declare it; the *Shastras* elaborate it; the *Gita* and other sacred texts describe how to experience this truth. Develop faith in the *Atma* and in the *Shastras*. They are the two eyes which will help you to gain the vision. Do not let this chance go to waste by clamouring for sitting space, causing confusion, and disturbing those who are engaged in listening. This is tragic when good things are spoken, you find it difficult to pay attention, but when demeaning, distracting things are spoken, the ears are on full alert. Well, listen quietly now and maintain this calm.

PLANT THE SEEDLING OF DEVOTION IN THE MIND

Man should be the master of his behavior. He should not be led away by the impulse of the moment. He must be conscious always of what is good for him. He should so carry on his daily tasks, that he does not make others suffer, or suffer himself. That is the sign of intelligent living. You should not give way to fits of anger or grief, elation, or despair. The confusion you exhibited now was the result of *Thamasik* (dark and dull), and *Rajasik* (emotional) qualities. Be *Sathwik*, calm, unruffled and collected. The more you develop charity for all beings, contrition at your own faults, fear of wrong, and fear of God – the more firmly established you are in *Shanthi* (peace).

INDIA IS THE 'HEART' OF HUMANITY

The very name *Bharath* is derived from the two words, *Bha* (Bhagavan-God) and *Rathi,* (the attachment to) *God*). That is why *India* has the role of the 'Teacher of the World'. She is also known as the 'Heart of Humanity' and is revered as such by seekers. But how can those who are starving feed others? It is your duty to sow and grow, and store and feed the world this great spiritual sustenance laid down in the *Vedas* and the *Shasthras*.

In this spiritual sphere of mental peace and inner joy, the responsibility for success and failure is entirely one's own. You have no right to shift it on to others. The fire will go out if the fuel is over, so stop feeding it with fuel. Do not add fuel to the fire of the senses. The negative *Shakti* (power) and the positive *Shakthi,* both together will give the light. Plant the seedling of *Bhakthi* (devotion), namely the preliminary exercise of *Namasmarana* (remembering the Lord's name) in the mind. That will grow into a tree with the branches of Virtue, Service, Sacrifice, Love, Equanimity, Fortitude, and Courage. You swallow food, but you are not aware how that food is transformed into energy, intelligence, emotion, and health. In the same way, just swallow this food for the Spirit, this *Namasmarana*, and watch how it gets transmuted as virtue and the rest, without your being aware

THE REAL TEST OF THEISM

Ravana discovered that *Ram*a and *Kama* cannot co-exist in the mind. Develop steadiness in the recitation of the name of God and in the worth of that Name. Then, even if the whole world says, *"Do Evil",* you will refuse to obey. Your system itself will revolt against it, and even if the whole world asks you to desist, you will insist on doing right. You must cultivate four types of strength, Strength of Body, Intellect, Wisdom and Conduct. Then you become unshakeable; you are on the path of spiritual victory. Once a person came to Me and argued that there was no God, and he was not prepared to believe in one. Well, I asked him "Have you faith at least in yourself? Which is yourself? Your Self is God. You have faith in your judgement, your intelligence, your ability because God within you, tells you not to falter or fear. That assurance wells from within, from your basic truth which is otherwise called God. It is enough if you believe in yourself. That is the real test of '*Theism*' I told him.

LISTEN TO THAT VOICE

I say the same thing to you also. The body is the Temple of God, in everybody. God is installed whether the owner of the body recognizes it or not. It is God that inspires you to good acts, that warns you against the bad. Listen to that voice. Obey that voice and you will not come to any harm. A lady wept that her necklace was lost or stolen. She searched everywhere and became inconsolably sad. Then when she passed a mirror, she found the lost necklace around her neck. It was there all the time. Similarly, God is there, as the inner dweller, whether you know if or not.

PARARTHA

There are three kinds of Love: *Swartha* or Self-centred, which like a bulb illumines just a small room; *Anonya* or Mutual, which like the moonlight spreads wider but is not clearer; and *Parartha* or Other-centered, which like the sunlight is all pervasive and clear. Cultivate the third type of Love, that will save you. For all the service that you do to others through that love, is in fact service done to yourself. It is not the others that you help, it is yourself that is helped, remember.

TWO WAYS OF REMEMBERING
THE LORD'S NAME

You might have heard me speak about *Namasmarana* and its fruits, how it slowly changes character and modifies conduct, and mellows you, and takes you nearer the Goal. Well, there are two ways of doing this; with a *Japa Mala* (*Rosary*), turning the beads automatically around just as mechanically and punctually and as carefully as any other routine act of daily life; or, as it ought to be done – repeating the name, irrespective of the target number, dwelling deep on the form it represents and on the divine attributes connoted by it; tasting it, reveling in it, enjoying the contexts and associations of the name, relishing its sweetness, lost in its music. Of course, you will be hankering after the taste of the name only when you are gnawed by the pangs of hunger. When you suffer from constipation as a result from over-indulgence in worldly affairs, you cannot relish the name or the form.

START NOW!

The mind is the mischief-maker. It jumps from doubt to doubt. It puts obstacles in the way. It weaves a net and gets entangled in it. It is ever discontented. It runs after a hundred things and away from another hundred. It is like a driver who drives the car with the master inside it, wherever his fancy takes him. So, take up the task of training it into an obedient servant. It is educable if only you know how to do it. Place before it things more tasty, and it will hanker only for those. Once it realizes the value of *Namasmarana*, it will adhere to that method of getting peace and joy. So, start it now. That is my *Ajna* (command) to you today.

Bhagavan Sri Sathya Sai Baba Udumalpet February 2ⁿᵈ, 1961

7

BE GRATEFUL TO
THE DOCTORS

Though I have been coming to this city for over twenty years now, this is the first time I am speaking to a gathering of the people living here. This time, the need and the deed must coincide, and today they have. This *Guru Poornima* has provided all three, and collected together in this sea of humanity, the waters of many areas through many channels and tributaries. *Mysore City* has earned fame by its devotion to music, sculpture, and other fine arts. But there is an art finer than all these, the *Art of Living*. Many a person skilled in other fields is a failure insofar as this art is concerned. He lives miserably, without a trace of joy, or contentment, or peace. He knows only pain, and he gives others only pain.

Mysore is also famous for the fragrance of its sandalwood. So far so good, but I would like the fragrance to emanate from your feelings, thoughts, and deeds, not so much from the trees that grow in the forests. Only then is the fame fully deserved. If the sense of beauty and the sense of harmony are not translated into the daily life of men, women, and children, then that life is a waste, a burden, a hoax.

Man must lift himself from the animal level through his own *Sadhana*. There are three types of men: the *Pashavi* (animal type), *the Sahaja* (human type), *and the Divya* (divine type). Since the beginning of creation, man has evolved from the stone through plant and tree, worm and insect, bird and mammal, but some are still grovelling in the early stages, though they have achieved the human form.

THE WORLD IS AN ENORMOUS HOSPITAL

Chief Minister Jatti, said that you are all like boulders, rough and hard, and that *Bhakthi* (*devotion*) has the power to make you soft and smooth. Now, what does a sculptor do when he sees a good boulder? He pictures in his mind the lovely idol of God that is sleeping inside it. He becomes possessed with the idea of liberating the idol from the hard clasp of the stone. He takes up his chisel and removes the extra stone that lies around the beautiful figure, and finally he liberates the image. The boulder has to suffer all that hard chiseling in order to become the image of God, so too you should cast off all the impediments, all the encumbrances that drag you down, and make you a boulder, instead of a *Bhaktha* (devotee) and a *Paramahamsa* (ascetic of the highest order), *or even Paramatma* (the Supreme Being).

The world is a huge hospital and humanity is bedridden. Some are writhing in the pain of envy; some are bloated with pride. Some are losing sleep through hate; some have become blind through miserliness. Some are struck down by selfishness, everyone has some illness or other. On this *Guru Poornima Day*, you must render gratitude to the doctors who diagnose your diseases and prescribe remedies, and the nurses who tend you back to health. You should also resolve today to follow the treatment recommended, and the regimen ordered. It is not enough if you learn the prescription by heart or read the label on the bottle three times a day or visit the hospital every day. Praising the doctor, or worshipping him, might induce him to take pity on you, but your illness can be cured only by your taking the drug, and obeying the restrictions on food and drink, and on your habits.

While talking of doctors, I must also say that doctors who fight for the patients' purse, or who try to grab a patient before a rival appropriates him, are a danger to society. The doctor who despises other doctors or sticks with his own patent cures irrespective of the experience of failure, or who is guided more by his whims, fancies, and prejudices, or who considers the patients' caste rather than his disease as more important; such men are very dangerous. Today, we find doctors and gurus who have deteriorated to the level of wrangling for patients and their purses, and for the sale of their own, or other people's remedies.

VYASA IS THE GREATEST OF
SPIRITUAL DOCTORS

This day is a day when mankind pays homage to the greatest of spiritual doctors, *Sage Vyasa. Vyasa* is the greatest of such doctors, for he put together the *Vedas* and composed the *Puranas* and the *Mahabharatha and* gave humanity the *Bhagavatha.* He is the primal Guru for all who walk in the Path of God. He planted the seeds of *Theism* and nurtured it through *Sruthi, Smrithi, Shasthra,* and the *Mahabharatha.* He gave the world the *Gita* and the *Brahma Sutras,* the idea of the Atma, (the immanent soul), the story of the *Divine Leela,* (the secret of his changeful creation). He belonged to the era of about 3800 BC. *Vyasa* was the great-grandson of the *Sage Vasistha,* the son of *Parasara,* and the father of that celebrated gem among *Rishis, Suka.* His life-story is a series of miracles: A Divine Saga. He came from *Vasudeva,* announced the *Leela* of *Vasudeva* to all, and finally, got merged in *Vasudeva.* He established the era of *Namaparayana* (*repeating and discoursing on the Lord s Name*) and made all aware of the sweetness of the name of the Lord, which evokes His form and His Grace.

THE PRAYERS TO BE OFFERED DAILY

Vyasa first revealed to man the secret of making the mind as clear and full of cool rays, as the moon on a full moon night. That is why this *Poornima* is associated with him and with all *Gurus.* Today, every *Asthika* (who believes in God) must refuse to be content with a feast and a lecture. He should try to plant today the *Nambija* (seed of the Lord's name) in his well-prepared heart, devoid of the thorns of egoism; and water it with *Prema* (love), fence the sprout with *Shraddha* (faith), feed it with the fertilizer of *Smarana* (remembering the Lord's name), and from the grown-up tree of the *Mantra* (sacred formula), pluck the fruit of *Ananda* (bliss), and relish the sweetness.

A person may boast of the vast treasures in the vaults of his bank, but he will get credit only for that which he has already earned and deposited therein. Do not fritter away the time allotted to you. Offer it to *Kesava,* who is *Kalaswarupa* (time personified). Know that waking from sleep is birth, and going into sleep is death. On waking, pray every morning of your life:

"Oh Lord I am now born from the womb of sleep,
I am determined to carry out all tasks this day as offerings
*   to Thee,*
With Thee ever present before my minds' eye.
Make my thoughts, words, and deeds, sacred and pure
Let me not inflict pain on anyone

Let no one inflict pain on me
Direct me, guide me, this day"

And when you enter the portals of sleep at night pray:

"Oh Lord The tasks of this day whose burden
I placed on You this morning, are now accomplished.
It was You who made me think, speak, and act,
I therefore place at Thy Divine Lotus Feet,
all my thoughts, words, and deeds.
My task is done. I pray to you to receive me
I am coming home to You".

Adopt these as your daily prayers. The best thing is to have your own Self as the source of light, as the *Guru*. The inner intelligence, the inner Guru will reveal the truth. This prayerful attitude will so educate your impulses, that the inner intelligence will be fully revealed.

DO EVERYTHING WITH A
SPIRIT OF DEDICATION

Begin with the cultivation of *Prema* (love). I have found that the people of *Karnataka* have great faith and devotion. They are simple in their thoughts and habits. Do not allow these to decline; cultivate them with care. The Chief Minister said that all are children of the Lord. It is better to say that all are actors in the drama designed by Him, dolls dancing and acting, as He pulls the strings. The role you have, might be that of an officer, a soldier, a revolutionary, a beggar, or a priest. Act well your part so that the drama might be a success. Do everything in a spirit of dedication, as if in each moment you act, speak, and even feel, in response to a command received. To get that mood of dedication, the *Bhakthi Sutras* (aphorisms on devotion) prescribe nine paths, but the easiest and the most practicable is *Sramana* (a life lived in the constant remembrance of the Lord).

DO NOT BE LIKE A GRAMOPHONE

A bar of iron sinks in water but beat it into a hollow vessel and it will float merrily and even carry some weight. So too, man's mind sinks easily in the sea of senses. Beat it hollow, hammering it with the name of the Lord, and it will float safely on a sea of troubles. Do not be like a gramophone record singing someone else's song, ignorant of the genuine thrill of music. Sing from your own experience of the Glory and Grace of the Lord.

If you win the Grace of the Lord, even the decrees of destiny can be overcome. There are certain drugs which come in bottles on which the manufacturer has given an ultimate date beyond which the drug loses its efficacy. Of course, the drug will be in the bottle but would no longer be effective. Similarly, the Lord's Grace can make it inoperative.

The Guru is One Who Shows You the Path for Getting That Grace and To Such a One This Day is Dedicated.

Bhagavan Sri Sathya Sai Discourse Guru Poornima Mysore July 27th, 1961

8

GO BEYOND THE ILLUSION

I had no plan till now to speak to you, but *Kasturi* mentioned that those of you who are here for many years, have not had the chance of even a *Namaskaram* (reverential salutation) for three months, (i.e. from before *Shivaratri,* when streams of devotees started coming in). He stated that you are all hungry for *Darshan*, since I am spending hours and hours talking with those devotees who are anxious to leave this place. I put in My Appearance at the *Bhajan Sessions*, twice a day, just for a minute or so, to receive *Arati* (worshipful ceremony of lights) and leave. I find you are all sad at what you misinterpret as neglect, so I shall administer some tonic to your drooping hearts. Well, you have the chance to see, experience, and be sanctified by the incarnation of the Lord. This chance you have got, as a result of the accumulation of merit in many previous lives. That merit has brought you here when I have come down. For this chance *Rishis* (Sages) and *Dhevas* (Demi-Gods) have prayed long in the past. Having won this chance, strive to taste the sweetness, and achieve the bliss of merging, without wasting even a single moment.

The Rays that emanate from me, are of three grades.

1. * The *Sthula* (physical, gross) filling this *Prasanthi Nilayam.*
2. * The *Sukshma* (the subtle) pervading the Earth.
3. * The *Karana* (causal) covering the entire Universe.

The people who have the privilege of living in this *Nilayam* are indeed lucky, for they are nearest to the *Kirana* (Rays).

The *Sthulakirana* makes man a *Sadhaka*, The *Sukshma* makes him a *Mahatma* (*Great Soul*) The *Karana* converts him into a *Paramahamsa* (*Ascetic of the Highest Order*).

Do not therefore waste your days entertaining worldly desires and ambitions and planning to achieve them. Success in this line, or failure, should not elate or depress you. When a banquet is in store for you, why run after the droppings from others' tables. Such plans and desires have no finality or fixity. They have no genuine worth.

COMMAND THE MIND AND REGULATE YOUR CONDUCT

Keep undimmed before you the main goal, the task for which you have come into this school. Do not deviate from it whatever the attraction that tempts you to stray. Command the mind, regulate your conduct so that the goal is won. Let not the care of the body, nor the fostering of the family, nor the demands of pride and pomp overwhelm the call of the Spirit for Self-expression. *Shiva* (Supreme reality)*, Jeeva* (individual) and *Prakriti* (subjective world) are the three principles that confront you. The world must be utilized by the individual to attain *Shiva,* which is the fundamental fact in both. Until you get *Athmanandham* by realizing *Shiva*, the world will press on you with its weight and well-nigh suffocate you. When you realize God, the world will finally vanish, as you discover the bliss of your spiritual truth.

Winning the Grace of the Lord is as easy as melting butter. That is why the Heart of the Lord is compared to butter; it is as soft as butter, they say. A little warmth is enough to melt it. A little warm affection shown to a suffering companion; a little warmth while pronouncing His Name, turning it over on the tongue, so to say. The sacred name of God is the spring of all the *Chaitanya* (essence of the Supreme Spirit) which you get by *Namasmarana*. It is the life-giving nectar; it is the fountain of primal energy. Recite the name, and the named will be before you. Picture the named, and the name will leap to your lips. They are the reverse and the obverse of the same coin, the name and the form.

BE STEADY, FIXED IN YOUR RESOLVE AND CONDUCT

There are some who vow to write *Ramanama* or some other name, a million times, but very often it's just a matter of the fingers and the pen. The mind of the writer is the spoon which does not taste the honey which it doles out. The mind should not wander from the name. It should dwell on the sweetness which the name connotes. It should ruminate on the beauty of the form which it recalls, the perfume which it spreads. The conduct and behavior of the writer should be such as befits a servant of God. Others should be inspired by them, and their faith should get freshened by their experience of the writer.

To earn the goodwill of the master, there is one recipe; obey his orders without murmur. I am telling you My Truth, not in Self-praise, but so that you can understand Me. If I do not speak about Myself, who can?

Grace is showered on all who obey instructions and follow orders, but the number of such is very small. Even though instructions are light and easy, they are designed to make you go beyond *Thriputi* (the three-fold distinction of the pilgrim, the path, and the goal) of *Bhagavatha, Bhaktha, and Bhagavan* – of lover, loved and love. You are in *Ambaresha Thatwa* (principle of devotion) one moment, and in *Dhurvasa Thatwa* (principle of anger), the next. This is wrong. You should be steady, fixed in your resolve and in your conduct. That is why, outside the *Prashanti Nilayam,* I serve in my discourses what you call *Vindu* or feast, but here, to you, I always administer *Mandu* or drugs. This is the *Kendram* (the centre), the headquarters of the *Asthika Army* which is to establish *Lokakalyanam* (world prosperity). Of course, I insist everywhere on piety and a high moral life, but here, I lay down stricter and more rigorous rules. Well, I shall tell you some hard words. You very often condemn the mind as a Monkey, but take it from Me, it is far worse. The monkey leaps from one branch to another, but the mind leaps from the heights of the *Himalayas* to the depths of the sea, from today to ten thousand years ago. Tame it by the process of *Namasmarana*. Make it, as *Ramdas* (A Hindu Saint) did, into a *Bhadhrachala* – a stable steady mountain. That is the task I assign to you. Make your heart an *Ayodhya* by means of *Ramanama*. *Ayodhya* means a city that can never be captured by force. That is your real nature – *Ayodhya* and *Bhadrachala*. Forget this and you are lost. Install *Rama* in your heart, and then no outer force can harm you.

BECOME MASTERS OF YOUR OWN KINGDOM

Realize that like the waves of the sea, *Sukha, and Dhukha,* (pleasure and pain) rise and fall. They are like the inhalation and the exhalation of the breath. If you attain that calm, the ground whereon you stand becomes *Kashi,* every handiwork of yours gets transmuted into the highest form of *Shiva Puja.* Roam about in the region of your own mind and understand its moods and mysteries. Do not dream of wandering in foreign lands before you become masters of your own kingdoms. Self-first; Help-next. Know yourself; that lesson once learned, you can know others much sooner and much more truly.

DEDICATE THIS LIFE TO THE
SERVICE OF OTHERS

Dedicate this life to the service of others, for the others are only invisible representatives of the Lord who resides in you. I have come to repair the ancient highway leading man to God. Become sincere, skillful overseers, engineers and workmen and join me. The *Vedas*, the *Upanishads,* and the *Shastras* are the roads I refer to.

I have come to reveal them and revive them. The rules I have prescribed for those who come to the *Nilayam* may appear strict and even severe, but it is all for your good. Inner purity first and outer purity later – that is the natural order. You feel full satisfaction wearing washed clothes when you take a bath first. I must be strict with you. because if I excuse one error, the tendency is to immediately commit another. A plant will grow well only when the ground around the stem is raked up and exposed to the sun and rain. I want you to drag old deep-rooted habits of purposeless talk, vanity, envy, and scandalmongering. You are not to live like earnest *Sadhaka's,* just to please Me. It is a duty you owe to yourselves, and so, you must adhere to those rules wherever you are, not merely within the confines of the *Nilayam.* Of course, the *Prasanthi Nilayam* you will have noticed, has no wall or fence around it; for it is not limited by any boundaries, it spreads and spreads, until it envelops the Universe.

Generally, I speak sweetly, but on this matter of discipline, I will not grant any concessions. I do not care whether you come, or having come, go. I will insist on strict obedience. I shall not reduce the rigor to suit your level, for that will only ruin you. I pay attention to your ultimate good.

Live peacefully, happily, contentedly, taking each day as a gift from the Lord. Do not rush and scramble, fret and fume. Be vigilant, and do not allow greed, or anger, to creep in. Attend all the sessions in the Hall, the *Pranava Japa* (recitation of Om twenty-one times in the Mandir), the *Bhajans,* (devotional singing), and divine discourses. Do not take shelter behind excuses. If you are ill, *Bhajans* will help the cure, or let Me tell you, it is far better to die during the *Bhajans* with the Lord's name on the lips. *Sadhaka's* are led along wrong paths and the respect due to pious people is dwindling, because they are not kept rigorously on the hard path. Concessions have spoiled them. Hereafter, I will not excuse the slightest deviation. You have been here for years and so, I must treat you as grown-ups, not as children. It is on account of the *Prema* I have towards you, that I rebuke you when you take a false step. My *Anugrakarana* (Rays of Grace) will make the lotus of your heart blossom.

THE DISEASE OF BIRTH AND DEATH

In a hospital, the doctors care for the disease, not for the size of the bank deposits the patients have. Disease is the important thing. So too, everyone suffering from *Bhavaroga,* (the disease of birth and death) and the dual effects of good and bad, has a right for the care and consideration of the doctor. The doctor prescribes the drug and the regimen; both are supplementary. When you get a relapse of doubt and distress, take the drug a greater number of times, and in larger doses. Join *Satsang* (the company of the Godly). Just as the tamer of elephants' surround a wild tusked elephant, rope him, bind him hand and foot, and immobilize him, prior to taming him, the spiritually minded will similarly bring the doubter round.

The current flows always along the wire. You only have to make a connection and switch on. If the connection is loose, then the flow of grace will be disturbed, and might even stop. It is you that connects and disconnects. You switch on and off, and you get day and night. Study the *Gita.* You know the *Gita* draws a line which you should not cross. I do not ask for your vows. Why should I force you to make them, and cause you to break them?

If you do so, your life becomes a torn cloth; stitched loose; it may tear again at the slightest pull. Let me tell you one thing in the end; ***However You Are, You Are Mine. I Will Not Give You Up. Wherever You Are, You Are Near Me. You Cannot Go Beyond My Reach.***

Bhagavan Sri Sathya Sai Baba.
Prasanthi Nilayam April 28ᵗʰ, 1962

9

SPIRITUAL ACADEMY
OF HUMANITY

The study of sacred books and listening to religious discourses is meant to develop self-control and peace, but from the confusion here, which you seem to enjoy, I find that your study and listening have all been a waste. You cannot put forward as excuse the hugeness of the gathering, because if each one of you stops talking, or clamouring, or complaining, silence can be established that very second. Again, you cannot say that you have been waiting since early morning, and therefore you have become restless. Well, what is to be said of the earnestness that melts away, just when the event for which you have been waiting so long has started? If each one keeps silent, though there are lakhs of people here, it would appear as if there are none. Try to keep silent. Remember why you have come, and why you have waited, and to whom you have come to listen.

Now it is better. That is good. That is why I always say that man's real nature is *Shantham* (peace, equanimity), that if only he tries, he can discover his nature in a moment. He has only to pull himself up, to collect his origins from *Brahman*, his identity with the changeless *Atma*. Man may get lost in an uproar, or be right and calm in silence, as you are now. Your own enthusiasm has caused this delay, for the road to the *Mandir* (Hall of Worship) is, as the organizers say, completely packed. Even there in the *Mandir,* there is not a square of vacant space! So, it was suggested that the Idol could be brought to this bungalow for consecration. It could be taken later and placed in position at the *Mandir.*

DO NOT DISHONOUR THE HERITAGE OF INDIA

Remember, *Sai* does not live in structures of stone, or brick and mortar! He lives in soft hearts, warm with sympathy, and fragrant and universal love. Temples and image worship have some value in stimulating the higher impulses of Man, if diverting his instincts along more socially useful channels. That is why in India, no chance is lost to leading man Godward. All arts are utilized to that end. Even a drunkard sways to the tune of a faintly remembered *Keerthana* (music composition), proclaiming the Glory of God, or the joy of Self-Realization. Everyone, whatever the stage of spiritual advance he may have attained, is prompted, gently nudged to move forward. This has made India the *Spiritual Academy of Humanity*. You are privileged to live out this life in the lap of India; that is, in the lap of *Vedanta*. Remember this heritage and live in such a way that you do not dishonor it.

Do not envy the countries that are attempting to reach the Moon and Mars, and to explore the reaches of outer space. To what avail is it to master those regions, while remaining slaves of every gust or fear? To what avail is it to travel at ten thousand miles per hour, with a mind weighed down by dark impulses of a savage past? Inquire into the causes of *Ashanti* (lack of peace) that prevails even in the most advanced communities of the West, and you will find the reason to be the growth of pride and greed, vice and sin. They attach meaning and value only to the external symbols of riches or power; the container, not the thing contained. For example, this marble image is only a container. The thing contained is *Sai Thatwa* (essential nature). Just as a cup is the *Adhara* (base support), and the milk within it is the *Adheya* (supported), you pour *Sai Thathwa* in this form, and you call it *Sai Baba*; you pour it in another vessel of a different form and call it *Srinivasa,* or *Shiva, Krishna* or *Rama.*

IDOL WORSHIP

For those in the kindergarten of *Sadhana,* an idol is as necessary as pictures in a spelling book. Until you can recall instantly the images of a horse as soon as you see the letters H.O.R.S and E, one after another, the drawing of a picture must be held before you with those letters underneath it. So, also, you must have a form like the idol, called *Sai*, prominently before you, to give shape to your loose and indefinite conception of the *Divine Thathwa* (true state). Once you can conceive the *Sai Thathwa* independently, without any form, or as all forms and names, the idol is superfluous, it can be dispensed with.

Installing this marble image in the *Mandir* yonder, does not mean the end of all effort for you, in fact, it is just the beginning. There are a large number of temples all over this country in various stages of ruin. Not only here, but in other countries also the same thing holds true. Why make all this noise and build another temple to be added to the list? New temples rise and old temples fade from memory and fall into decay. This is because you do not realize the substance is the same, though it is presented in different forms and under different names. One chapter of your

Tapas (penance) is finished; you have now got this idol, and you have organized the ceremony, but the next chapter is to pour your *Bhakthi* into the idol and make it ever alive, to shape your own lives, so that you are fit to stand before *Sai* with folded hands. Only the pure and the holy can offer themselves fully to God.

DO YOUR BEST FIRST AND SEEK GOD'S HELP

I do not like people wasting the precious moments of their limited years of life in idle talk of vain pursuits, not do I like cowardly hesitation. Act! Act with all your might, and with all your mind. Make full use of the skill, capacity, courage, and confidence that you are endowed with. Then *God* will bless you. You must have heard of a *Ramabhaktha* (devotee of *Rama*), who sat on the roadside by his upturned cart. *Rama* did not appear to raise the cart and fix the wheel. Wailing his bad luck, and calling on *Rama* to lift the cart, he therefore, began chiding his faith itself and doubted the experience of the sages who describe Him as the *Ocean of Mercy*. *Rama* came into his presence then, but only to tell him: "*You Fool! I have entrusted you with some intelligence and strength. Use them! Put your shoulder to the task now before you. When you have done your best and that best is not enough, then call on me. I am ever ready to reinforce your exertions with My Grace.*" The *Bhaktas' of Rama* with His Name on their lips and His Form before their eyes, lifted mountains and bridged the sea. You who call yourselves *Athmabhakthas* are too weak even to carry about your bodies, not to speak of the burden of your kith and kin.

YOU MUST GROW IN PREMA-LOVE

Having installed *Sai* in your village, you must grow in *Prema* (*love*) *for: Sai is Premaswarupam* (love personified) *Sa– means*

Sarvashakthi (all-powerful) *Sarvasakshi* (the witness in all), *Ayi* means Mother, *Baba* means Father. The Love of *Sai* is *Prema*, characteristic of *the Father* and *the Mother*, not the earthly father and mother, but of the Divine parents of every being. Respect the father and mother who are real, and then you transfer that type of respect to the abstract father, mother or guardian-God who is the witness of every thought, word, and deed. Learn to realize the unseen Lord in your heart by installing the visible image in the *Mandir*. Proceed from the *Sthoola* (gross) to the *Sookshma* (subtle).

DISCOVER TRUTH BY EXERCISING DISCRIMINATION

Just as patients require a Doctor, *Bhaktas'*, require some name and form to which they can run for consolation, courage, and advice. So, it is for your sake, as a great step in your *Sadhana* in your progress towards internal peace and harmony that this installation is made by Me now. It has been said
"Wherever My Name is Sung, there I install Myself."
The divinity you have as the core of your being, you ignore. At the same time, you seek it in others. That is the tragedy. You insult yourself by feeling helpless, weak, and inferior. Cowardice, and self-condemnation, – these do not become a spark of the divine flame. Your *Sathya* (truth), can be discovered by you, by a little exercise of *Viveka* (discrimination). Born in delusion, breathing in delusion, grovelling in delusion, man is unaware of his heritage, and feels incapable of attaining it. He is desperate, seeing no means of escape. Every effort to achieve *Shanthi* (peace) entangles him further and tighter in the coils of *Ashanti*. Like flowers of variegated hue, each redolent with fragrance, men are all basically of the unique name of *Brahman*. The fragrance arises from the divine essence, which is the real

reason for existence, for everyone must realize that essence, and thus end the series of births and deaths, like a student leaving college, once the degree is awarded. Once the truth is realized, man has liberation. He can leave his college and his study and all that bother.

You must rely on your own resources, but you must get the degree! Why are you averse to making the effort needed to pass? Instead of that, you run after this teacher or that. You extol him to the sky and call yourselves his followers. To what avail is his victory to you? He has achieved! Well, what about you? His achievement is entered in his account at the bank, as his deposit, and he can draw cheques upon it, but can you draw from it? There are even today great Sages in the *Himalayas,* I know, who are witnesses of everything and whose *Prema* embraces the whole of humanity, but that does not help you. You have to trek the path alone and rely on your own resources. They can provide only guide maps and encouragement. You have come to *Repalle* today from the hundred distant villages, and you know that you must go back to the places from where you came. So, too, it is inevitable that you must return to the place from where this journey through birth and death started, namely *Brahman.*

There is only one Sun, but he is reflected in a million tanks and wells and pots. *Paramathma* (God) is One, and His reflections are the *Jeeva's* (individuals), each with the *Atma* (Soul) apparent therein. There are lakhs of people here now, and in each one of you now, *Swami* is shining in the heart. That is the real *Athmanandham* (soul-full bliss). Keep it fresh forever and foster it carefully. That is the secret of *Shanti* (peace).

Installation of Bhagavan Shri Sathya Sai Baba Idol
in the Mandir Repalle December 2ⁿᵈ, 1961

10

GOD – THE DIVINE TRINITY

'Man's foremost duty is to make the stream of Divine Love
   flow throughout the World.
It is not for living for himself, that every man has been
   born.
Only by having the noble thought that he has to serve society
   will he ennoble himself and achieve self-satisfaction.
Of what avail is human birth, if you cannot get rid of
   narrow feelings and resolve to serve all mankind.
What greater message can the Guru give?'

EMBODIMENTS OF DIVINE LOVE

Forgetting God, his inherent eternal divinity, man today regards
Life as intended only for the pursuit of selfish aims. It is this
divinity that should be manifested in man's life. Creation is the
projection of Divine Will. It is called *Prakriti* (*Nature*). In every

object emanating from nature, the divine principle exists and must exist. It is to proclaim this immanence of God, that man has evolved. Consciousness in nature is not purposeless. When it is filled with ego, it gets deformed. When it is turned towards the Atma (soul), it becomes divine. To whom is this consciousness to be dedicated? It is certainly not for egoistic ends. It should be offered to God; however, man today is caught up in so many selfish pursuits, that he has degraded himself to the level of animal and is displaying demonic traits. At every step, he is violating *dharma* (righteousness). Every desire is turning into greed. Generosity is on the decline. Man's vision has lost the light of love. Truth is a casualty in man's speech. Spirituality has become a form of ostentation. Qualities *like Kama* (lust) and *krodha* (anger) are having a free rein. Consciousness has become dormant in man. Human relationships have become mechanical and artificial. In fact, humanness has virtually disappeared.

WHY DOES GOD INCARNATE?

In this situation, what is it that man should seek? How can he attain peace and happiness? The first pre-requisite is the cultivation of the love of God. The *Puranas* and the ancient sages have declared that God incarnates to punish the wicked and protect the good. This is not correct. God incarnates to inculcate love in mankind, and to teach how love should be promoted and practiced. Only when such love is developed, will man be free from sorrow and trouble. Sins will be wiped out and fear will cease to haunt men.

When there is love of God, there will be fear of sin. When both are present, society will experience morality. Man's primary duty is to foster these three: *Daiva Preeti, Papa Bheeti, and Samaja Neethi* (love of God, fear of sin, and morality in society). This must be done by developing *devotion* (*bhakti,*) on the basis of faith and love. Actions have to be performed with devotion. Love is Devotion. The faith generated by love is *jnana* (knowledge). The actions done based on love and faith are *Karma*. The combination of *jnana* and *karma* leads to *Upasana* (worship). *Upasana* is the combined outcome of *bhakti, jnana* and *karma.*

DEVELOP LOVE TO EXPERIENCE BLISS

The dualistic attitude is rampant in man today. Dualism can never eliminate sorrow. It can only increase it. It takes man far from bliss. Therefore, it is essential to cultivate the sense of *Oneness* (Ekatwa). Love alone signifies that Oneness. For this Love, there is no path, no reward, no discipline, other than love itself. The more you develop this Love, the more you experience bliss. Today, love is limited and polluted. It is limited to one's kith and kin. Our love should transcend these narrow limits, embrace the whole world and extend to every living being. Love is present in everyone in varying degrees. In nature, everything functions according to its specific qualities.

The *Upanishads* declare: *Swabhavasthu Pravarthate* (everything behaves according to its specific nature). It cannot be altered or destroyed by anyone. This is the inherent attribute of nature. It manifests the divine principle, which is eternal, immutable, and unchanging. To bring out this divine aspect in Nature, and make it manifest, all things have been endowed with certain *qualities* (Gunas). *They are Satwa* (purity of the mind), *Rajas* (passion)*, and *Thamas* (ignorance). To endow nature with these qualities, certain media are necessary. These have been described as *Brahma, Vishnu,* and *Maheswara.*

THE GUNAS AND THE TRINITY

Brahma, Vishnu, and *Maheswara* are not entities with forms. The trinity represents the deified expression of the three qualities. The *Puranas* have misrepresented *Brahma* as a four-headed deity engaged in cosmic creation. This is not correct. In fact, the Trinity represents the three *Gunas.*

There are five elemental powers in Nature: *Bhoomi, Apa, Agni, Vayu, and Akasha* (earth, water, fire, air, and space or ether). If you want to understand the process of creation, the order of description of these elements must be reversed. Starting from *Akasha* (space), we have in succession air, fire, water, and earth. Nature must be understood in two ways: one in relation to the process of creation, the other in relation to the everyday experience. Likewise, when the order of *Brahma, Vishnu,* and *Easwara,* is viewed in relation to creation, it must be reversed; we have *Easwara, Vishnu,* and *Brahma* in that order.

To begin with, what does the Principle of *Easwara* signify? The *Gita* declared:

'*Easwarasarvabhootaanam   hriddese   Arjuna   thishtathi*' (O'Arjuna, *Easwara* dwells in the heart region of all beings.) *Easwara,* therefore means the Lord of the Heart. He illumines the heart of every being. This means that the divine power of *Easwara* is present in every heart. The other name given to *Easwara* as Lord of the Heart is *Atma.*

THE SUPREME GURU

It is from the heart that the spirit has emerged. The spirit corresponds to the *Vishnu principle. Vishnu* means One who is All-Pervasive. The spirit is equally All-Pervasive. '*Manomoolam idam Jagat*' it is said. *The spirit is the basis of the cosmos;* hence it signifies the *Vishnu principle.*

Brahma is traditionally described as arising from the navel of *Vishnu*. It is from the mind that *speech* (Vaak) has come. *Vaak* is the embodiment of *Brahma*, hence *Brahma* has, among other names '*Sabda Brahmamayee* (sound is *Brahman*). Thus *Easwara, Vishnu,* and *Brahma,* symbolize the heart, the mind, and the faculty of speech. The combination of all the three represents the *Atma.* Each of the three should be revered as one *Supreme Guru* in three forms.

> *"Gurur-Brahma Gurur-Vishnu,*
> *Guru Devo Maheswara*
> *Guru Sakshat, Parabrahma,*
> *Thasmai Sri Gurave Namaha"*

This sloka, which has profound and sacred significance, has been given a distorted meaning, elevating the role of the ordinary teacher, fragmenting God, and missing the basic truth of Oneness expressed in it:

> *Gurur-Bhahma* – The *Brahma* referred to here is not the creator; it refers to *Vaak* (*The word*)
> *Gurur-Vishnu* – refers to the all-pervasive mind, which is present in all beings. This is the *Vishnu* principle.
> *Gurur-Devo Maheswara* – refers to the seat of the Heart.
> *Gurus-Sakshar-Para Brahma*
> *Thasmai Sri-Gurave Namah*

This means that the unity of speech, mind, and heart represents the *Supreme Atma,* which should be revered as *Guru* (inner master).

THE GUNAS AND THE COSMOS

What is the role of the *Guru*? It is the total removal of the darkness of ignorance. As long as there are the three *gunas,* there can be no freedom from darkness. It is only when one transends the three *Gunas,* that one attains the state of the *Guru.* Alternatively, when one realizes the unity of the three *Gunas,* the message of the *Guru* is comprehended. The importance of the unity of the three *Gunas* is indicated in the *Gita* declaration: '*Mamatma Sarvabhootatma*' (My Atma is the indwelling spirit in all beings). That which dwells in all beings is the only One). (*Eko Vasi Sarvabhootantaratma*) (the one that is the inner spirit in all beings).

Forgetting this basic principle of Oneness, and lost in the wilderness of multiplicity, man is having no peace. It is on account of the varied functioning of the three *Gunas*, that the process of creation, growth, and dissolution, can take place. The three *Gunas* are the primal source, the basis, and the life-breath of the universe. They are responsible for the manifestations and transformations in nature. The permutations and combinations of the three *Gunas* in varying proportion, account for the infinite diversity in the Cosmos.

THE TRINITY AND THEIR
CORRESPONDING COLOURS

Three colors have been ascribed to the three *Gunas'*. It is commonly believed that *Vishnu* represents the *Sathwa Guna*. It is not so. The *Sathwa Guna* is really the attribute of *Easwara,* it is not subject to *Maya*. In the state of *yogic sleep* (Yoga Nidra), it acquires the *Chith-Shakthi* (the power of awareness) and appears as *Suddha-Atma* (the pure absolute). Hence, *Sathwa* represents the *Easwara* principle. Its color is white. The *Rajo*

Guna manifests itself in likes and dislikes. It used to be associated with *Brahma*, but this is wrong. It is a quality associated with *Vishnu*. *Vishnu* has been depicted as a deity bearing the conch, the discus, the mace and the lotus. *Vishnu* has also been described as *Alankaraswarupa*; (One who is embellished by decorations). *Vishnu* also bears the name; *Viswambhara* (One who protects and rules over the Universe). As a ruler (*Raja*), he has the *Rajo Guna*. The color of *Rajo-Guna* is red.

Then there is *Brahma*. The *Rajo Guna* has been attributed to *Brahma*. This is incorrect. *Brahma* represents *Thamo Guna*. *Thamo Guna* is associated with *Murkhatvam* (irrationality) and *Andhakara* (the darkness of ignorance). It is filled with *Mamakara,* (the sense of possessiveness) *and Abhimana,* (attachment). These two impulses account for creation. If there were no sense of 'I" and 'Mine', the creative process would not go on. These two are the insignia of *Thamo Guna*, which is represented by the color Black. White, red and black are the most important colors. All colors are merged in these three. Likewise, there are in the world, people with *Satwa Guna, Rajo Guna,* or *Thamo Guna,* and are distinguished by one or other of the three colors.

FIVE KINDS OF SADHANA

What is the way to bring about unity in this diversity of colors? The ancient sages, after deep enquiry, have indicated five different paths for achieving this objective. They are *Sathyavathi, Angavathi, Ananyavathi, Nidanavathi,* and *Swarupatmaka-Jnanam.*

Sathhyavathi is a kind of *sadhana*. This *sadhana* reveals the presence of God in a subtle form everywhere, in everything, in the same way butter is present in milk. The sadhana provides the proof for the view that God is the Universal In-dweller abiding in all beings. No one should think that God dwells in a particular place or in a particular being.

76

The purpose of this *sadhana* is to make one realize that God is present in all beings, and to act on that conviction.

Next is *Angavathi Sadhana*: This discipline represents the five elements in the Cosmos: *Space, Air, Fire, Water, and Earth.* God is present in each of these elements in a specific form. In *Space* (*Akasha*), God exists in the form of sound as '*Om*'. The form of *Pranava* (Om) emanates from *Akasha*. *Air* (Vayu) has the power to sustain life. This power is represented by hydrogen and oxygen in the atmosphere. Oxygen has this divine life-sustaining potency. God is thus present in air in the life-giving breath (*Prana*). This is a matter of daily experience for everyone. When somebody faints, the people around him are cleared, so that he may have more air and breathe more freely. This is a recognition of the presence of the life-energy in air.

In *Fire*, God is present as an alarm-signaler. Even when a fire is mild, people are careful. Consciously, or otherwise when we must deal with fire, we have a sense of cautiousness. In *Water*, God is present as *Prajna* (integrated awareness). The scriptures declare: *Prajnanam Brahma;* integrated awareness is *Brahma.* This *Prajna* arises out of water. When a person becomes unconscious, water is sprinkled on him to restore consciousness.

The fifth element is the Earth (*Prithvi*). In Earth, consciousness (*Chaitanya*) is present. The potencies present in the Five Elements: *Prajna-Sakthi* (integrated awareness), *Jagrata-Sakthi* (the awakening or warning potency), *Chetana-Sakthi* (consciousness), *Sabda-Sakthi* (the potency of sound) *and Jiva-Sakthi* (life-sustaining potency) are all different forms of the divine power. Those who are engaged in the *Angavathi sadhana* regard the five elements as manifestations of the *Supreme Paramatma* and offer worship to them.

The third sadhana is *Anyavathi*. In this discipline God is worshipped based on certain insignia in a particular form like that of *Vishnu* or *Shiva*. *Shiva* for instance is envisaged as a deity with three eyes, the Trident, a *Damaru* (Tambourine), and He is worshipped in this form. Similarly, *Rama* is pictured as One bearing a *Kodanda* (a bow), and *Krishna*, as the Lord with the flute, wearing a peacock feather on his head. In this manner each Deity is distinguished by certain special insignia for purposes of worship.

Next is *Nidanavathi*. This is the common type of sadhana practiced by most people today. It comprises nine types of worship practiced by devotees: *Sravanam, Kirtanam, Vishnusmaranam, Padasevanam, Vandanam, Archanam, Dasyam, Sneham and Atmanivedanam.*

The fifth *sadhana* is (*Swarupatmakam Jnanam*). This discipline aims at achieving the realization that every individual is an embodiment of God and hence, God is present in everyone. The *Gita* declares: '*All feet are His, all eyes, heads and mouths are His.*' That means, all human forms are divine. True education should enable one to realize his inherent divinity.

We speak often about prayer. Prayer does not mean petitioning to God. Prayer is a fraction of the experience of *Atmic Bliss*. It is a means of sharing this bliss, spreading it all around, being immersed in that bliss. Prayer must come from the heart. Prayer that is not heartfelt is utterly useless. The Lord will accept a heart without words, but he will not accept words and prayers that do not come from the heart. This is why God is described as the Lord of the heart, (*Hridayesa*). It is only when you have faith in this, that you will be able to manifest your divinity.

See the body as a temple in which the Trinity – *Brahma, Vishnu and Maheswara* reside. There are no separate places where *Brahma, Vishnu,* or *Easwara* dwell; like *Vaikunta* or *Kailas*. These are delusions born of ignorance. God is inside you, outside you, around you. You must recognize this truth and live according to it. *Chittibabu* (who had addressed the gathering earlier), referred to persons who are attacked by doubts all the time. As long as you are filled with doubts, you cannot experience peace or happiness. We must perform all actions with the firm belief that – We are God and God Is in us. We must experience this sense of *Ekatwam* (Oneness).

FROM UNITY TO DIVINITY

What is the use of all the sadhana you are doing? Only when the underlying unity of the *Satwa, Rajo* and *Thamo-Gunas* is recognised, can you experience the bliss of Self-Realization. For realizing the *Atma* (Self), there is no need to go to any place. Do not imagine that God comes from somewhere to give you *darshan*. What need is there for One who is Omnipresent to go from place to place? God is beyond coming and going.

Realize the importance of unity. To achieve unity, you must cultivate purity. When you have purity, you realize divinity. You have only 'community' in the sense of 'mine' and 'thine'. You must develop fraternal feelings without regard to barriers of race, religion, caste, and class. When you develop this sense of kinship, nations will progress and prosper.

In the name of *Guru Poornima*, you perform some pujas for some person and waste your lives. There is only One *Guru* – He is God. That *Guru* is within you. You are seeking the *Guru* all over the world. Your qualities (*Gunas*) are in you, in the form of *Brahma, Vishnu,* and *Maheswara,* and can protect you, elevate you, or ruin you. When you act righteously and pursue the right path, they will protect you by their Divine Potency. Neither sin, nor God have any separate existence from you. Our actions and thoughts assume the forms of sin, or merit, as the case may be. The royal road to happiness and the removal of sorrow is right action. The essence of all religions, all teachings, and spiritual paths, is only one thing – love. Develop that Divine Love.

NEVER GIVE GOD UP

Above all, whatever your difficulties, whatever the ordeals you have to undergo, in any situation, do not give up on God. God is One and All. Whether you are affluent or destitute, whether you are scholar or ignoramus, whatever troubles you may be faced with, whatever spiritual practice you may adopt, whether you are regarded as a sinner or a saint – Do not give God up and realize that *God is One and All.*

*From Bhagavan's Discourse in The Poorna Chandra
Auditorium on Guru Poornima Day July 29th 1988.*

"Prayer is a very powerful weapon, far more effective than any bomb.
The word is an effective tool. It can move mountains.
In these critical times, all of us should pray deeply and sincerely for the peace and prosperity of Bhaarata Maatha (Mother India)".

Sathya Sai Baba

11

THE DIVINE PRINCIPLE

All living beings emanated originally from water. Humans have bodies built out of food based ultimately on plants sustained by water. Speech is the special acquisition of human beings, and the earliest use man made of this talent to utter the Glory of God and pray for his Grace is the RK (rik) of the (Rg) *Rig Veda*. The RK was rendered enchanting, because it attributed names to God, while paying homage to the Supreme. All such names are subsumed and treasured in the sound *Om,* the audible, but not visible sign and symbol.

THE PRANAVA SOUND

O*m* is God Himself*,* the *Paramatman,* the *Cosmic, and Trans-Cosmic Consciousness.* Every moment, in every cell, in every atom, the Om resounds, reverberates and activates. *Om* energizes, sustains, and fills the Universe. *Om-Ithi Ekaksharam*

Brahma (the single word *Om,* is indestructible, it is *Brahma*) assert the Upanishads. The *Vedas* assure us '*Ayam Atma Brahma*' this *Atma* (Soul) is Brahma. The sages were aware that the *Atma* is *Om,* even when they defined *Om* as *Brahma.* In fact, all the three expressions indicate the One and only Entity.

THE FOUR PHASES IN THE EVERYDAY LIFE OF MAN

Everyone must achieve the awareness of the *Atma* within him. Man passes through four phases of life every single day. He is awake (*Jagrath*), he dreams (*Svapna*), he sleeps (*Sushupthi*), and he reaches the phase beyond the three (*Thuriya*). When awake the person is involved incessantly with the objective world, through the senses. The eyes can distinguish colors; the ears welcome good and bad sounds; the tongue tastes and rejects; the nose gathers information about fragrant and forbidding smells. The basic attributes of the Five Fundamental Elements (*Ether, Wind, Fire, Water and Earth*) are apprehended by the five senses as *Sound, Touch, Form, Taste,* and *Smell,* in that order. So, in this waking state the individual is concerned, not only with himself, but with all the Cosmos around. Therefore, the waking stage is called *Viswa* (global). The Soul of man then assumes an Omnipresent form reminiscent of *Vishnu,* the director of sensual activities, the *Hrshikesa:* (The controller of all worldly life).

During the phase of dreams, man returns to himself. The senses of perception and action, rest and sleep. During this time, he is busy with his memory, and the plans and projects the mind has played with. Even people sleeping adjacent to one another dream differently, according to each one's tendencies and mental mysteries. The dream has validity only for the dreamer; it absorbs light from the deeper levels of consciousness. It reveals the soul, through its inner luminosity.

1. So, the first stage is therefore called *Thaijasa,* part of the nature of *Thejas;* (shining with the light of the soul).
2. During the second stage *Sushupthi,* (deep sleep), the senses, the faculty of reason, and the mind are all out of action, and are re-integrated into the Self.
3. In the third stage, the person is unaware during sleep, of himself or others, but he can recall every detail as soon as he wakes. During sleep, he is merged in consciousness, pure and simple. So, the phase is named *Prajna.*
4. The fourth stage is *Thuriya,* where the person is aware of the divinity that is his nature. He merges with the *Absolute* or *Samadhi.*

THE FOUR ASPECTS OF PRANAVA

The Sound *Om* (*Aum,*) *known as Pranava,* also has four parts or stages.

1. The Sound '**A**' (as in *Manna*) is a basic sound in speech and is universally utilized. It is parallel to the *Viswa,* or wakeful phase of man's daily life.
2. The sound '**U**" (as in put) is indicative of the breathing process (inhaling and exhaling) which ensures the glow of vitality or *Thejas.* The breath persists in the dream stage and so it corresponds to the dreaming phase.
3. Then we have the '**M**' sound in Om, (as in Am), which closes all externalizing and internalizing outlets and inlets of consciousness, and enables man to be alone with his *Reality, Prajna, or Brahma.* So, it symbolizes the condition during *Sushupthi* and can be defined as the *Prajna* phase.
4. The silence into which the Om tapers is the consummation, the *Thuriya* phase, when the veil of ignorance that has prevented the ecstasy of *Brahman* from illumining the awareness is removed, and one is conscious of the mergence.

THE COSMOS IS BRAHMAN

The *Atma* is associated with speech, breath, and mind in the body, though it remains unaffected. It is a spark of the all-comprehensive *Brahman*, the all-pervasive *Om*, which is ever-present. Brahman is defined as being *Sath* (Awareness), *Chith* (Consciousness), and *Ananda* (Bliss). When it is said that education must result in the manifestation of the divinity already in man, it is the awareness of the *Atma*, that is indicated as the goal. When *Sage Narada* approached *Sanat kumara* for spiritual guidance, he was asked by the *Guru,* to relate what he had learnt up to that moment. The credentials had to be laid bare.

Narada reeled off a long list of subjects and texts that he had mastered. He was happy that *Sanat kumara* was listening to him with attention. When he finished, *Sanat kumara* described the entire list as mere *'names'* of things, and ideas, names devoid of substance. He told *Narada: "Discourse is more meaningful and weightier than name. The mind from which speech springs is more significant than speech; the will is more fundamental than the mind; Consciousness is the prompter of the will; both depend on vital energy which is derived from food. Food is grown on earth with the help of water; the element water is a derivative of fire, which itself is a by-product of air; and air is a manifesto-tion of space, the first projection of the will latent in Brahman. Therefore, unless you know Brahman, your knowledge cannot be total and completely satisfying"* This teaching of *Sanat kumara* reveals that the Cosmos is *Brahman* in complete totality, and that *Om* is activating it as the *Cosmic Sound*. Matter is saturated with God, every molecule of it. Though matter is the product of becoming, it is still a genuine fragment of the divine being that has become matter. Hence it is that we can see it, deal with it, and recognize it, as a whirl of energy. Energy, latent or patent, greater or less, exists in all things. It is the divine characteristic within all.

Contemplation on God and on the symbol *Om* resounding in us with every breath and reminding us of the One which persists in us during wakefulness, dream, and sleep, can ensure the awareness of the *Sath-Chith Ananda* we really are.

(Bhagavan Sri Sathya Sai Divine
Discourse December 30ᵗʰ1986)

12

LIGHT THE LAMP OF LOVE IN YOUR HEARTS

On the evening of 22ⁿᵈ June1967, Bhagavan inaugurated the new wing of the official hostel residence of the students of the institute of Sathya Sai. Then in the refectory residence, especially decorated for the occasion, He addressed the students and all the teaching staff. Here is the discourse He delivered:

"A lamp has a unique power which is not possessed by any other object. It dispels darkness. For this reason, *Bharatiya's* have always worshipped lighted lamps. Before commencing any auspicious or religious function, the ceremonial lamp is lit. Another notable quality of the lamp is that the flame goes upward, the path of the *Brahman*. The sinful path leads downwards. The light of the lamp, however, can only dispel the darkness outside, but cannot remove the darkness that envelops the heart because of attachments and aversions carried from previous lives. Not all the blaze of light which filled *Lanka,* when *Hanuman* set it on fire, could remove the darkness from *Ravana's* heart. Because his heart was filled with lust or hate, no light could penetrate it.

Even as a lamp needs a container, oil, wick, and a matchstick to light it, for lighting the inner flame, one needs a container in the form of renunciation (*vairagya*), *bhakti* (the oil of devotion), the wick of mental concentration, and the matchstick of *tathwajnana* (true-awareness). Even if any of these four are missing, the light of the Self cannot be lit."

WHO WORKS FOR ME ONLY?

The world today is immersed in fear and suffering. The only way to get rid of fear is to cultivate non-attachment (*Vairagya*). Where there is no attachment, there is no fear. Only through non-attachment and renunciation, can one acquire the competence to experience inner illumination. Renunciation does not mean giving up property and society and taking oneself to the forest. What is called for is renunciation of all evil tendencies. That is *Yoga*. (union with God).

In the *Gita*, three paths have been indicated by Lord Krishna:

1. *Mathkarmakrit: He who works for me only*
2. *Mathparamo: He who looks on me as the only refuge*
3. *Madhbhaktah: He who is devoted to me*

Here, *Mathkarmakrit* (*He who works for me,*) does not mean doing service to *Krishna*. The '*Me*' represents the *Cosmic Being*. Because everything in the universe is permeated by God, each one is enjoined to do service to all, as the primary duty. All actions must be done in society. You must serve your country. The individual, the community and the world are the triune aspects of divinity. To ignore any one of these is to court failure in the purpose of living. The goodness of the individual promotes the welfare of society. Social well-being is the basis for national welfare

CURB YOUR DESIRES

The cultivation of *Vairagya* (renunciation) calls for practice of certain restraints and disciplines. There should be curbs on desires. One should give back to society what one has been able to acquire using knowledge, and skills received with the help of society. True sacrifice consists in sharing with others, one's wealth, strength, and qualities, which are in fact derived from society.

One should not be remiss in discharging one's duties and responsibilities. The proper fulfilment of duties is part of the spiritual discipline necessary for getting enlightenment. No room should be given for doubts. Many are haunted by doubts of every kind. While doubts remain, there can be no liberation from bondage.

BECOME KARMA-YOGIS

Students should strive to lead exemplary lives. No one can completely give up all social relations or actions. Hence, one should dedicate all actions to God and thereby develop the sense of detachment. To remove the chaos and violence prevailing in society today, you must become *Karma-yogis* and devote all your knowledge, abilities, and energies to the transformation of society. It is not wealth that is important. Character alone counts. *Bhoga* (sensual pleasure) can only lead to *Roga* (disease). *Thyaga* (sacrifice) leads to *Yoga* (communion with God).

Today, in this residence, I have lit the lamp of love like a symbol of spiritual light which should light up the hearts of any of you. Spiritual illumination is as vital as academic knowledge. All other branches of knowledge are like rivers which fuse with the ocean of spiritual knowledge.

YOUR LIFE MUST BE AN EXAMPLE TO OTHERS

During your educational career, develop purity of character, and cultivate right habits. Even in ordinary routine actions like sitting, do not be sloppy and indifferent. If your back is bent when you sit, the *Sushumna Nadi* (the energy which runs through the spinal column) gets bent, and this will produce harmful consequences including loss of memory power. Discipline is vital. Avoid unnecessary talk and purposeless association with anyone. Having come for study, you must concentrate on your primary duty. Strive to make your parents happy by your conduct and performance and see that you bring credit and good name to the institute. Only then will your life be an example to others.

Bhagavan Sri Sathya Sai Discourses at the Inauguration of The New Wing of the Sri Sathya Sai Students Institute Hostel, June 22nd, 1987

"Today, in This Residence, I Light This Lamp as A Symbol of The Spiritual Lamp Which Must Illuminate the Heart of Each One of You."

13

MEDITATE UPON AND REPEAT THE NAME OF GOD

I have come in response to the prayers of sages, saints and sad-hakas. The *bhaktha* (devotee) who spoke first here now, was, let me tell you, denying God for 25 years and it is only for five years, after seeing me, that he has changed. Of course, many people have had no experience which could change them, and so they are not to be blamed for their want of faith. So too, this *Seshagiri Rao* here was finding fault with his son and daughters for coming to *Puttaparthi*, and with himself for long refusing to come! One day at Bangalore, there was a function at the house opposite to his, for I had gone there. During *bhajans* (singing of devotional songs in groups), this man hesitantly crossed the road and peeped into the hall, and I went forward and called him and made him sit near me. I asked him to come to *Puttaparthi* and invited him to *'examine and experience'*. He has been with me ever since. It is now 18 years since he first came here.

This is just the reason why I came to sow the seeds of faith, in religion and in God. You might have heard some people say that I became *Sai Baba* when a scorpion stung Me! Well, I challenge any one of you to get stung by scorpions and transform yourself into *Sai Baba*! No, the scorpion had nothing to do with it! In fact, there was no scorpion at all! I came in response to the prayers of sages, saints, and Sadhakas (spiritual aspirants) for the restoration of *Dharma* (righteousness).

When there is a sign of a little unrest, the police constable appears on the scene. If the mob gets unruly, the inspector rushes in; and if it becomes violent, the police superintendent needs to be personally present on the scene to quell it. If, however, the situation becomes hot, the inspector general must make himself available, is that not so? This is a situation in which the inspector-general is taking over-all charge of the situation. The *Mahapurushas, the Mahatmas,* the *Jnanis,* the *Yogi's,* and *Divine Personalities,* have done what they had to do, and they will all be co-operating in the task of re-establishing righteousness and clearing the path for the world attaining *Santhi* (absolute peace)

THE ATMA – VICHARA

The greatest defect today is the absence of *Atma Vichara*, the enquiry into the nature of the *Atma* (soul). That is the cause of all this *A-Shanthi* (restlessness). If you are eager to know the truth about yourself, then even if you do not believe in God, you will not go astray. The pots are all of mud, the ornaments are all of gold, the clothes are all of yarn. There is unity where one saw only diversity; the basic substance is One and indivisible. *Brahman* is the supreme reality; it is also the *Atma* (soul) which is your own basic essence.

This *Atma Vichara* is best found in the *Upanishads*. Just as a river's flow is regulated by bunds (embankments) and the flood waters are directed to the sea, so too, the *Upanishads* regulate and restrict the senses, the mind, and the intellect, and help one to reach the sea, and merge individuality into the *Absolute*. Study the *Upanishads* with a view to act accordingly, to put the advice into practice. Scanning a map or turning over a guidebook will not give you the thrill of the actual visit, nor will it give you a fraction of the joy and knowledge of a journey through that land. The *Upanishads* and the *Gita,* are only maps and guidebooks, remember this.

LOVE OF GOD TRANSCENDS TIME AND PLACE

There is the story of a rustic who sat among a gathering of devotees and listened to the exposition of the *Gita* by a great pundit. All were wonder-struck by the scholarly commentary and learned disquisition on every word and phrase which the pundit gave, and although the exposition was very much over his head, the rustic seemed to attend very closely for he was all the time in tears! When at last the pundit asked him why he was weeping, he surprised everybody by the sincerity of his *bhakti* (devotion). He explained that he wept at the predicament of the Lord, who had to sit at the head of the chariot and half-turning His Neck, held forth so long to convince the dull-witted Arjuna. *"O! How much he must have suffered; he must certainly have had pain in His Neck?"* he asked and wept. He had identified himself with the participants in the episode, and the whole setting had become alive for him.

CALL UPON THE LORD WHO IS
IN YOUR OWN HEART

You need not even read the *Gita,* or the *Upanishads.* You will hear a *Gita* specially designed for you, if you call upon the Lord in your own heart. He is there, installed as your own charioteer. Ask him and he will answer. Have the Form of the Lord before you when you sit quietly in a place of meditation and have his name when you do *Japam*. If you do *Japam* without that picture or form before you, who is to give the answer? You cannot be talking all the time to yourself. The *Rupam* (form) you have chosen will listen and will manifest to you to reply to your prayers. All agitations must cease one day, isn't that right? The *Dhyana* of the Form, and the *Japam* of the Name, (the meditation on the Lord's Form and repeating His Name) – are the only tools to accomplish this task.

THE LORD HAS TO ASSUME THE FORM YOU CHOOSE

The secret is: you should 'be', but 'not be', just as in sleep, when you are conscious, you are aware deep down within you, that you exist. In fact, sleep is enveloped in *Maya* or illusion. Wake-up and get out from this *Maya* (Illusion) and immerse yourself in the sleep which is true *Samadhi* (the state of super-consciousness and bliss).

Japam and *Dhyanam,* are the means by which you can compel God's Grace to assume the form and the name you yearn for. The Lord must assume the form you choose, the name you cherish; in fact, you shape Him so. Therefore, do not change these two, but stay faithful to your ideal, whatever the delay or the difficulty. If at the very beginning you are not able to concentrate for very long, do not get discouraged.

When you learn to ride a bicycle, you do not acquire the skill of keeping balance immediately. You push the bicycle along to an open road, and hop and skip, leaning now to one side and then to the other, and even fall with the bicycle on top of you on many an attempt, before you can ride with skill, never again to have to worry about balance. Automatically, you can make the necessary adjustments to correct the balance, isn't that right? After accomplishing this skill, you can ride through the narrow streets and lanes, and you do not even need an open road, you can negotiate your vehicle through the most crowded thoroughfares. Likewise, it is practice that will equip you with a concentration to sustain you in the densest of surroundings and the most difficult situations.

WHEN YOU MEDITATE

Do not be under the impression that I will be angry with you if you do not choose this form of *Sathya Sai Baba* as the *Dhyanarupam* (the form of God you choose to meditate upon)! I am not concerned at all; you are perfectly free to choose the Form you love the most.

- During your meditation, the mind jumps from one thought to another and takes a different path to the one you are following.
- Therefore, you need to guide it along the two rails of name and form, so that the flow of your thoughts with the Lord is not interrupted.
- If the contact is lost, you should quickly return to the name and the form.
- Do not allow the mind to go beyond the twin embankment paths, this side *Nama* (name), that side *Rupam* (form), so that it docs not stray into a third path.
- Initially when you sit for Meditation, recite a few *Slokas* (sacred prayers on the glory of God), so that all thoughts that are scattered can be recollected.
- Then little by little, as you are continuing to repeat the sacred name (*Japam*) internally visualize, the form which that name represents.

- During this repetition of the name, if your mind wanders away from the form, call it back and order it to recite the name you have chosen.
- When it wanders away from the form, lead it back to the name. Let it dwell either on this sweetness or that. Treated thus, it can be easily tamed.
- The imaginary picture you have drawn, will be transmuted into the *Bhavachitram,* the emotional image dear to your heart and fixed in the memory.
- Gradually it will become the *Sakshathkarachitram*, the form assumed by God to fulfil your secret desire.

This *Sadhana* (spiritual practice) is called *Japasahithadhyana,* (meditation on the form and name of God). Therefore, I advise you all to take it up, for it is the best for beginners. Within a few days, you will taste the joy of concentration. In the initial stages, after about ten or fifteen minutes of this meditation, dwell on the *Manama* (inward contemplation) of the *Santhi,* and *Sowkhya* (peace and contentment) you had during the *dhyana.* That is to say, recall into your memory the joy you experienced. This will help your faith and earnestness. Then, do not get up suddenly and start moving around, resuming your tasks. Loosen the limbs slowly, deliberately, and gradually and then enter upon your usual duties. Taste the fruits of *Dhyana* and learn to enjoy them. That is what I want to say when I speak about the process of *Manana* (repeated reflection or visualization).

YOUR BODY IS THE PERFECT
VEHICLE TO REALIZE GOD

Be careful about your physical health also. Satisfy the demands of nature. The car must be given the petrol which it needs; otherwise, your head might reel, and your eyes might get blurred through sheer exhaustion. How can thoughts of the Lord be stabilized in a weak frame? When you take care of your body, do not forget its purpose. A road-roller is fed with oil and coal and other types of fuel. But why is it kept in good trim? In order to mend the road, isn't it? Similarly, remember that you have become embodied, so that you might realize the end of this cycle of birth and death. For that sake, use the body as an instrument, that is all.

Flying hither and thither, higher, and higher, the bird has at last to perch on a tree for rest. So too, even the richest and the most powerful man seeks rest, *Santhi* (peace). *Santhi* can only be found in one shop, the shop of your inner reality. The senses will drag you along into a mire which submerges you deeper and deeper into alternate joy and grief, in other words, you will feel continually dissatisfied. Only the contemplation of unity can remove fear, rivalry, envy, greed, desire, all the feelings that prompt dissatisfaction. Every other practice can only give pseudo-contentment. A day will come when you will throw away all these play-things and toys, crying "*Lord, grant me divine peace*". Like the brigand *Valmiki*, the confirmed atheist will also one day have to pray for peace and rest.

People hug brass pots and take them to be gold, but they have to polish them, so that they appear bright. One day, they will get disgusted with this constant polishing and scrubbing; they will pray "*Release me from this scrubbing, this birth, this suffering and this agony*". Life is short, time is fleeting, your *sadhana* is creeping at tortoise speed. When will you decide to proceed a little faster? You *sadhana* is like the answers you write at the examination. If you only get 5 or 6 marks, then the examiner will strike out even that, saying "What is the use of these few marks; it will neither take him here, nor there"

If you get somewhere near passing marks, then grace will give you just a little more, so that you may pass, provided you have been a diligent well-behaved student.

ENGAGE YOURSELF IN GOOD
THOUGHTS AND ACTIONS

Engage yourselves in good deeds, good company, and good thoughts. Fix your attention on the goal. You have not shared yet the secret of this advent. You are indeed lucky, more fortunate than many others. It is only when *Yashoda* found every length of rope a little short to go round His belly, that she discovered He was the Lord. So too, you will realize every description of *My Mahima* (Divine Glory) a little too short of the actuality; and then you will get convinced. Meanwhile, if you study the *Shastras* and know the characteristics of the *Avatar of the Lord*, you might get a glimpse of the truth regarding Me. There is no use arguing and quarrelling among yourselves, Examine, experience, and then you will know the truth.

EXAMINE AND HAVE YOUR OWN EXPERIENCE

Do not proclaim before you are convinced. Be silent while you are still undecided or engaged in evaluating. Of course, you must discard all evil in you before you can attempt to evaluate the mystery, and when faith dawns, fence it around with discipline and self-control, so that the tender shoots might be guarded against the goats and cattle, the motley crowd of cynics and unbelievers. When your faith grows into a big tree, those very cattle can lie down in the shade that it will spread.

Bhagavan Sri Sathya Sai Discourse Chitravati River-bed,
Puttaparthi February 23rd, 1958

14

SRI RAMA – *THE NAME THAT REDEEMS*

There is no Bharatiya (Indian) who has not heard the story of Rama, nor is there a village in Bharat without a Rama Temple. From time immemorial, every individual in Bharat has regarded Sri Rama's life as an ideal and has sought to sanctify every moment of his life by living up to it. Bharat has always considered the life of any one devoid of spirituality, as utterly valueless.

Sri Rama Is the Very Embodiment of Righteousness

Sri Ramachandra was born on a day when the planet *Sukra* (Venus) enters *Meena* (Pisces). The month of his advent marks the beginning of *Vasantha Ritu* (Spring). It is the time when the sun enters *Mesha Rasi* (*Aries*). *Sri Rama's* incarnation as a human being was for the purpose of promoting peace and happiness in the world. *Ramo Vigrahan Dharmah* (*Rama* is the very embodiment of righteousness). It was as if righteousness itself had incarnated on earth. *Dharma* and *Rama* are inseparable. *Rama's* life falls into two parts: the earlier and the later. In the earlier part *Rama* figures as the heroic warrior who vanquished powerful persons like *Parasurama, Vali, and Ravana. Rama* excelled not only in physical strength, but also in intelligence and character. It is impossible to describe all the virtues of *Rama.* Every *Avatar* has six types of Power: *All-encompassing Prosperity, Righteousness, Fame, Wealth, Wisdom, and Renunciation* (or non-attachment). God is the sole possessor of these six attributes. *Sri Rama* had all these six attributes in equal measure. Every *Avatar of God* in every age and every place has these six attributes.

TRUTH AND RIGHTEOUSNESS

In the *Ramayana, Sathya* (truth), and *Dharma* (righteousness), are the most important concepts. The *Vedas*, which are regarded as their very life breath by *Bharatiyas*, have proclaimed: *Sathyam Vada; Dharmam Chara* (speak the truth: act righteously). In order to honor the plighted word of his Father, *Rama* elected to go to the forest leaving *Ayodhya.* Truth is the foundation for all righteousness. There is no greater religion than truth. *Rama* stood out as the upholder of truth, to fulfil the promise of his father, to maintain the traditions of his *"Ikshvaku Dynasty"* to protect His country, and for the sake of the welfare of the world. Everyone who calls himself a human being should stand up for truth in the same manner. It is said of high-souled men (*Mahatmas*) that what they speak, what they think, and what they do are in perfect accord. In the case of the wicked, their thoughts, words, and deeds, are at variance with each other. By these definitions, *Rama* was a *Mahatma* (a high-soul), and *Ravana* was a *Duratma* (an evil-soul).

THREE WOMEN AND THREE GUNAS

In the first twelve years of *Rama's* life, he encountered three types of women. When He accompanied the *Sage Viswamitra* to the forest to protect His sacrifice, He encountered the Ogress *Thataki*. He put an end to her without any compunction or aversion. After *Vishwamitra's* sacrifice was completed, *Rama* went with the *Sage* to *Mithila*. On the way, He came across *Ahalya*, who had been transformed into a stone. He gave her life, absolved her of sin through penitence, and restored her to her husband. At *Mithila*, He encountered *Sita*. He accepted *Sita* without any hesitation. What is the inner meaning of these three incidents? They show that even from His boyhood, *Rama* displayed extraordinary qualities and stood out as an example to the world. *Thataki*, the first woman He encountered, symbolizes the *Thamas* quality. He destroyed the *Thamasic* quality, *Ahalya* represents the *Rajo Guna*. He taught the right lesson to *Ahalya*, purified her, and sent her home safely to her place. He took to Himself *Sita*, who represented the *Sathwic* quality. *Bhagavan* approves of and accepts only that which is *Sathwic*. He values the *Sathwic* quality. He protects and fosters it.

Today all the three *Gunas, Thamas, Rajas, and Sathwa* are present in man in varying proportions. What does the presence of the *Thamo Guna* signify? It is natural for the Thamasic person to regard un-truth as truth, wrong as right, evil as good. Although the phenomenal world is impermanent and illusory, the *Thamasic*-minded person regards it as permanent and real.

The *Rajasic* person lacks the power of discrimination and yielding to likes and dislikes, behaves without restraint. Impulsive action is characteristic of persons in whom the *Rajo Guna* is predominant. Because of hasty and impulsive action, they are subject to all kinds of difficulties. In the process, they waste their lives. People should try to avoid acting in haste. Haste makes waste, waste makes worry, so do not be in a hurry. In the quest for God, there should be no hurry. Purity and serenity are required for God realization. There can be no happiness for the man who lacks peace. *Saint Thyagaraja* said in one of his songs 'Without peace, there is no happiness'. *Thayagaraja* was a great devotee of *Rama*. As a devotee, he had numerous experiences which he conveyed to the world through his songs.

THE TRIPLE POWERS OF THE NAME OF RAMA

What are the inner meanings of the Name Rama? The three syllables *'R' 'A' and 'Ma'* indicate three causes for human birth namely: *'Papamu, Thapamu, Ajnanamu:'* the sins one has committed; the troubles one experiences; and one's ignorance.

> *Ra…. represents the root letter for Agni.*
> *Aa… represents the root letter for Moon.*
> *Ma… represents the root letter for Sun.*

What does *Agni* signify? It destroys everything and reduces it to ashes. The letter **R** has the power to destroy all sins committed by man. The letter *A* (symbolizing the Moon) has the power of cooling the fevers man suffers from and conferring peace on him. The letter **M** represents the sun who dispels the darkness of ignorance and confers the illumination of wisdom. Hence the word *Rama* has the triple power of destroying sins, conferring peace and dispelling ignorance.

When you utter the word **'Ram'**, you first open the mouth with the sound **Raa.** All your sins go out when the mouth is open. When you mutter **M** by closing the mouth, the entry is barred against the sins that have gone out. Everyone should recognize the sweetness, the sacredness, and the divinity enshrined in the name *Rama*. It was for this reason that *Thyagaraja* sang: *"Oh mind, contemplate on the Name of Rama, with full awareness of its* *power.* It is good to utter the name of *Rama*, with full understanding of all that it signifies, but even without that understanding, the chanting of the name has the power to destroy all sins.

CHANT THE SWEET NAME OF RAMA

We must learn to chant the sweet Name of *Rama* with a pure, unsullied heart, in a spirit of selfless devotion. In the mind of man dwell the deities representing the moon and the sun. Intelligence is endowed by the sun. However, two kinds of birds haunt the mind. One bird fosters the sense of *'I'* and *'Mine'* and fills the mind with ego. This is a destructive force. The second bird fosters the feeling of freedom from attachment and hatred. It signifies the power of the sun in the mind. *'Rama'* who belongs to the solar race, adhered to the latter path.

THE GLORY OF SPRING

There is a significant connection between the *Rama* principle and *Vasantha Ritu,* the season of spring. In spring, the trees offer new leaves and flowers and fill the world with gladness. When the sun's rays shine on the fresh leaves, they acquire a golden hue. The whole world puts on a glorious new look in Spring. The beginning of the new year is celebrated in many regions, by the preparation of special edibles made from the fruits of neem and mango trees. Eating this mixture reminds man that life is a combination of pleasure and pain, profit, and loss, and both are to be treated with equal mindedness.

In spring the air is full of the fragrance of mango blossoms and the song of the cuckoo (*Kokila*). There is joy in the air you breathe. The *Kokila's* (cuckoo) calls are never so sweet as in *Vasanth* (*Spring*). The *Kokila's* song is sweet to the ears.

If a crow sits on our roof, we wish to drive it away, but we welcome the *Kokila's* song. Why this difference? The crow seeks nothing from us. The *Kokila* has not given us a crown. The difference lies in their voice. The crows cawing jars on the ears. The *Kokila's* song is music to the ears. When the speech is sweet, the speaker becomes endearing. Hence, men should learn to speak sweetly and pleasingly. Sweet speech confers peace. It is the means to Self-realization. It is in the heart of the man who is sweet spoken, that *Sri Rama* loves to dwell.

THE LORD'S PERMANENT ADDRESS

Once the *Sage Narada* appeared before *Lord Vishnu* and said: *"Oh Lord, I move about in the three worlds, and I know the past, present, and the future. If I want to convey to you any special information, to what address should I send it? I do not want your temporary address. What is your permanent address?"*

Vishnu replied: *"Narada! Take down my permanent address: (Madbhaktah yatra gayanthi thathra thhishtami). Narada, wherever my devotees sing my Glories, I reside there"*

People ascribe various abodes for the Lord; *Vaikunta, Kailas, Badrinath, Kedarnath,* and so on. All these are only 'care-of' addresses. The direct address is only the heart of the devotee. As the *Gita* says 'The Lord dwells in the heart region of all beings. As the Lord is Omnipresent, He is equally in the heart of everyone. Hence the heart is described as *Atma-Rama,* one who delights the *Atma* (the soul) by His Presence.

OFFER YOUR HEART TO GOD

Whatever you do, don't do it to please others, but to pleasing the indweller in your heart, for your own inner satisfaction. This means acting according to the dictates of your conscience. Every such act will please God. To derive self-satisfaction from your actions, you must cultivate faith. When there is satisfaction, there is readiness for sacrifice. Through sacrifice, God is realized. Your faith should be unwavering, like that of the *Pandavas* faith, in *Sri Krishna.*

All spiritual aspirants and devotees like *Thayagaraja,* have had to experience many trials and tribulations. Even *Pothana,* the author of the *Telugu Bhagavatham,* was subjected to many pressures and ordeals, to compel him to dedicate his work to a local chieftain. *Pothana* stood firm because of his strong faith in *Sri Rama.* Rather than dedicate his work to a mere mortal, he was prepared to offer his heart and soul to *Rama. Pothana* totally surrendered himself to *Sri Rama* declaring: *"All that I have is yours. Whatever I receive or offer comes from you. I cannot claim anything that is mine own"*

Men go on pilgrimages to various holy places. When they are in *Benares,* they offer the *Ganga* water to the *Ganga,* uttering the names of the Lord. What is the special value of such an offering? You must offer to the Lord the heart that he has given to you. This is true surrender. *Lakshmana* is the supreme exemplar of the doctrine of surrender (*Saranagathi*). *'I offer my wealth, family and everything else to you, O' Rama. Protect me who has taken refuge in You"* It was this total surrender which compelled *Rama* to observe when *Lakshmana* lay stricken on the battlefield in *Lanka.* *"Wives and kinsmen can be found in any country, but where can one find a brother born from the same loins?"* *Rama* thus exemplified the depth of fraternal attachment. The mutual love between *Rama* and *Lakshmana* was of the highest order.

After the fall of *Ravana, Sugriva, Vibhishana* and others approached *Rama,* and appealed to Him to rule over *Lanka,* which was a richly endowed land. *Rama* turned down the request, saying that he could not give up His Mother, nor His Motherland. Even in this Devotion to the Motherland, *Rama* serves as an example to humanity. Today, everybody utters *Ram, Ram,* but very few follow the example set by *Rama.* They are not true devotees of *Rama.* At best, they may be described as *'part-time devotees.'* True devotion means perpetual remembrance of the name of the Lord and consistent meditation on the name, cherishing the figure of *Rama* in the heart.

FACE TROUBLES WITH FAITH

You should be prepared to face the vicissitudes of life with firm faith in God. It is during times of difficulties that God is remembered. To confront difficulties with faith is itself a spiritual discipline. Although *Rama* was the son of *Emperor Dasharatha,* and son-in- law of *King Janaka*, He had to face many ordeals in life for the sake of upholding *Dharma.* The *Pandavas* went through many difficulties for the sake of adhering to righteousness, and hence their name and fame remain forever. You should pray to the Lord to give you the strength to bear all troubles and face all difficulties. If you have even an atom of Grace of the Lord, a mountain of troubles can be overcome. *Chaitanya* declared: *"If a fraction of the time that is spent worrying about wealth, provisions, wife and children, friends and business, is devoted to contemplation on the sacred feet of God, one can face the messengers of death without fear and cross the ocean of Samsara!"*

CHANT THE NAME OF RAMA WITH LOVE

It is not necessary to devote many hours to prayer. It is enough if one thinks of God with all his heart and offers himself even for a few moments. A single matchstick when it is struck, can dispel the darkness in a room that has remained closed for years. Mountains of cotton can be burnt down by a single spark. Likewise, wholehearted chanting of the *Name of Rama* even once, can destroy mountains of sin. But the chanting should not be done mechanically like playing a gramophone record. It should emanate from the depths of the heart. Having been born in this sacred land of Bharat, having before you, the ideal example of the *Rama Avatar*, you must seek to redeem your lives by living up to *Rama's* ideals and proclaiming them to the world. Remember the Name of *Rama* with love. God can be realized only through love and by no other means. *Bhagavan* concluded His Discourse with the *Bhajan*: '*Prema Mudita Manase Kaho, Rama, Rama, Ram!*'

*Bhagavan Sri Sathya Sai's Discourse at Sai Sruti,
Kodaikanal on Sri Rama's Navami Day, April 14th, 1989*

15

LOVE OF GOD

One may be a Master of all the Scriptures
and Competent to teach the Vedanta
One may be a Great Ruler
Living in a Many-Splendored Mansion,
One may be a Valiant Hero
Who Has Vanquished his Enemies
or One may be a Pitiable Victim of Poverty and Privation.
If he has no Devotion in Him (Love of God)
His Life is Devoid of Meaning,
A Servant who is filled with Love of the Lord
Is more to be Adored, than the Overlord of the World

It has been said that *bhakti* is service to *Hrishikesa,* the inhabit-
ant of all hearts. Service to God has been described as *bhakti.*
The heart of the devotee flows with love of the Lord, through
constant remembrance and recitation of His Name. Out of this
stream of love, devotion emerges. One who is nourished by

the nectar of *bhakti,* will have no desire for anything else. To be unaffected by joy or sorrow, gain or loss, praise or blame; to remain steadfast and unwavering in faith, is the hallmark of true devotion. Affection, attachment, desire, are natural qualities in man. When these qualities are directed towards God, and when one is continuously engaged in good deeds; these qualities acquire purity and sacredness. Then a man becomes not only a great soul, but can become Divine.

PREMA ADVAITAM – UNITY IN LOVE

The devotee is ever conscious that the universe is a manifestation of God and is permeated by God. His life is based on the recognition of the immanence of God in everything. This state of mind is called *Prema Advaitam* (unity in love). Through this love, the devotee experiences his Oneness with God. Enjoying the bliss of this experience, the devotee does not even desire *Moksha* (liberation from birth and death). Unremitting love of the Lord is everything for him. Such devotion is known as *Ananya Bhakti* (total devotion to One and only One)

Bhakti (devotion) indicates that man needs, in addition to the *Four Purushartas* (the needs of life)*; Dharma, Artha, Kama, and Moksha*) a fifth object: devotion to God. Adi *Shankara* characterised this devotion as the mark of *Jnana.* There is no need to bemoan the fact that one has not been able to perform the prescribed rites or forms of worship. *Parama Bhakti* (supreme devotion to God) encompasses within itself all meritorious qualities.

LOVE OF GOD IS LIBERATION – MOKSHA

The *Puranas* consider *Moksha* (liberation) as mergence into God, but the bliss that is experienced by constant contemplation of God through devotion, cannot be achieved even by merging in God. *Vedanta* has claimed that love of God is *Moksha*. The heart of the devotee filled with love of God is tender and sweet. Sometime or other, everyone is bound to make his heart such a shrine of love for the Lord. With the Lord enshrined in him, the devotee denounces the desire for liberation. Devotion itself will make him One with the Lord.

When a drop of water falls into the ocean, it achieves immortality and infinitude. If you hold a drop of water in your palm, it evaporates in a few moments, but when you join it into the ocean, it becomes boundless and One with the vast ocean. Only through love can union with the universal be realized. To a devotee who has achieved such a union with the eternal, everything appears as divine.

The *Gopika's of Brindavan* were such devotees. They experienced divine bliss through their intense devotion. Like a fish that cannot live out of water, the devotee who is immersed in God, cannot relish any other thing. Every part of his body is so much filled with the nectarine ocean of divine love, he cannot exist for a moment without the love of God, and each organ finds expression in proclaiming the glory of God or rendering service to God. This was the kind of devotion the *Gopi's* had for *Krishna*. It was something beyond the intellect and the power for reason. *Krishna* explained to *Uddhava,* the true nature of the *Gopi's Bhakti*. Because such *Bhakti* is incapable of intellectual analysis, it is dismissed as blind faith. Intellectual enquiry cannot explore what is subtle and can be known only through experience.

ANAYA BHAKTI
TOTAL DEVOTION TO GOD

One day, a *Gopika* asked *Radha* how she felt when she first saw *Krishna*, how her heart responded, what transformation occurred in her and what joy she experienced? *Radha* replied: *"The moment I hear the melodious flute of Krishna, my heart becomes still, and I forget myself when I learn that Krishna is coming. I am lost in the music of His Flute, and I am aware of nothing else. How can I describe to you my feelings when I am intoxicated by the magic of his melody?"*

The God intoxicated devotee cannot describe his blissful experience in words. One who attempts to express it has no real experience of it at all. Those who regard themselves as devotees, should recognize the vast difference between their narrow-minded attitude, and the ineffable character of true devotion. They should resolve to shed all their petty attachments and develop steadfast devotion to God as the main objective of their life. For this purpose, the company of the good is essential. Good thoughts are promoted only through association with the good. This means avoiding contact with the evil-minded and the unrighteous. Association with bad persons makes even a good person bad. There are classic examples of evil consequences of association with the bad. *Kaikeyi* in the *Ramayana,* and *Dharmaraja* in the *Mahabharata,* are examples of persons who suffered grievously, because of associations with evil-minded persons – *Manthara* in the case of *Kaikeyi,* and the *Kauravas* in the case of *Dharmaraja.*

Everyone must strive to fill the heart with true devotion. Constant contemplation on the form of the Lord and frequent repetition of the Lord's Name is the means by which the heart is filled with inexpressible ecstasy. It was out of such ecstasy that *Kulasekhara Alwar,* the Royal Saint, exclaimed: *"Oh Lord, people talk of Moksha as the means of redeeming life and getting rid of birth and death. I do not ask for such redemption. I shall be content with loving You and serving You in countless lives. Allow me to Love and Serve You. That is the only blessing I seek from you, and not Moksha."*

SAGE NARADA'S PRAYER

The universe is permeated with Love. It is the embodiment of *Vishnu*. There is nothing in the Cosmos, no place in it where he is not present. To regard the universe as a manifestation of God and to experience it as such, is true devotion. *Sage Narada* was the supreme exponent of this doctrine. He observed: *Thayago bhavati thrupto bhavati, Atmaramo bhavati "The lover of God renounces everything. He is supremely happy. He is immersed in the bliss of the Self. Endow me with such love, Oh Lord"*

LOVE OF GOD DISPELS IGNORANCE

Man today, is behaving with less gratitude than those which birds, beasts, and even trees display. He is ungrateful to his parents, teachers, society and even to God. He makes a parade of his adherence to *Truth, Righteousness, Peace, Love, and Ahimsa* (non-violence), but does not practice any of them. Why is this so? It is because of intense selfishness and preoccupation with one's own concerns and interests. Only when man sheds his selfishness, can he turn his mind towards God. Love of God will dispel the ignorance and conceit of man, as the sun dispels the morning mist. The heart is the seat of love. That love must express itself, to begin with, in the home. From there it must extend to one's village or town, to one's state, nation, and ultimately to the whole world. Love must expand from the individual to the whole universe. We must regard love as God. The different forms attributed to God are products of fancy, but love can be directly experienced. Whether one is a theist, or an atheist, a hedonist, or a recluse, a yogi, or a materialist, he will have high regard for the cultivation of human love to achieve universal love. Love is the one form in which everybody is ready to accept God, the sublime path of *bhakt*i – that is the path of *devotion.*

THE PATH OF DEVOTION

To realize *Brahman* through continuous meditation on *Brahman,* is not an enjoyable path for all to take. This was why spiritual teachers like *Ramanuja* favored the path of devotion, experienced for themselves the bliss flowing from the love of God, and propagated the love principle as the easiest means to experience God. There have been teachers who have experienced the *Karma Marga* (the path of action), the *Jnana Marga* (the path of knowledge), and the different types of yoga, or other means to God. But the common under-current that flows through all of them is the path of *bhakti* – (The path of divine love). This is accepted by all of them. *God is Love. The Universe is permeated by God. To see God in everything, to love everything as a Manifestation of God to offer everything to God as an offering of love – This is the sublime path to Love.*

The *Gopika's, Sage Narada,* and the child *Prahlada* are supreme examples of the *path of bhakti.* Prahlada means one who is filled with infinite light. The delight with which Prahlada was filled, was for love of God. He saw God in everything. When his father *Hiranyakasipu* asked him whether God was in a pillar, he said God *was* in it. Hiranyakasipu smashed the pillar, and the Lord came out of it in the form of *Narasimha* (*Man-Lion*) to vindicate *Prahlada's* faith in the Omnipresence of God. Without firm faith in the Omnipresence of God, devotion has no meaning Without a strong belief in the Omnipresence of God, devotion cannot exist. By developing faith, devotion is nourished, and devotion enables one to face all the vicissitudes of life with fortitude and serenity, regarding them as dispensations of providence. Finally, one pointed devotion for God leads to union with God.

Today devotion begins with a kind of *yoga,* (morning ritual of worship), progresses at midday towards enjoyment (*Bhoga*) and ends at night with (*Roga*) disease.

The *Gita* says '*Satatam Yoginath*' – *Absorption in God is always the mark of the Yogi* (union with God). This cannot be achieved in one jump, but through constant practice, it *can* be achieved. Self-Realization is the goal and love is the means. It is through the cultivation of Love that life can find fulfilment. Everyone must strive to achieve this fulfilment, by filling this human adventure with the sweetness of Love and transforming it into an expression of Divinity.

This is My Blessing for All of you.

Bhagavan Sri Sathya Sai Baba Divine Discourse
at Abbotsbury, Madras January 19th, 1986.

16

WHO IS SAI?

God is inscrutable. He cannot be realized in the objective world. He is in the very heart of every being. Gemstones must be sought underground; they do not float in mid-air. Seek God in the depths of yourself, not in the tantalizing, kaleidoscopic nature.

The body is granted to you for this high purpose, but you are misusing it, like the person who cooked his daily food in the gem-studded gold vase that came into his hands as an heirloom.

Man extols God as *Omnipresent, Omniscient, and Omnipotent*, but he ignores His presence in himself! Of course, many venture to describe the attributes of God and proclaim Him to be such and such; but these are their own guesses, and the reflections of their own predilections and preferences. Who can confirm that God is this or that? Who can affirm that God is not of this form or with this attribute? Each one can acquire from the vast expanse of the ocean only as much as can be contained in the vessel he carries to its shore. From that quantity, he can grasp only a little of that immensity.

THE RELIGION OF LOVE

Each religion defines God within the limits it demarcates, and then claims to have grasped Him. Like the seven blind men who spoke of the elephant as a pillar, a fan, a rope, or a wall because they contacted but a single part of the animal and could not comprehend the entire animal. So too, religions speak of a separate part and assert that its vision is full and total. Each religion forgets that God is all forms, and all names, all attributes, and all assertions. The religion of humanity is the sum and substance of all these partial faiths. The various limbs of the elephant that seemed separate and distinct to the eye-less seekers of its truth, were all fostered and activated by one single stream of blood. The various religions and faiths that feel separate and distinct are all fostered by one single stream of Love.

*"There Is Only One Religion and That Is
the Religion of Love" Baba*

THE POWER OF SAI IS LIMITLESS

The eye cannot visualize the truth. It gives only false and fogged information. For example, there are many who observe My Actions and start declaring that My Nature is such and such. They are unable to gauge the Sanctity, Majesty, and the Eternal Reality that I Am. *The Power of Sai* is limitless. It manifests forever. All forms of power are present in this palm of *Sai*. But those who profess to have understood Me, the *Yogis* (spiritually advanced persons), the *Pandith's* (scholars), the *Jnanis* (the liberated sages), all of them are aware only of the least important, the causal external manifestation of an infinitesimal part of that power, namely the '*Miracles*'! They have not desired to contact the Source of all power and all wisdom that is available here at *Brindavan.* They are satisfied when they secure a chance to exhibit their book-learning, and parade their scholarship in *Vedic Lore*, not realizing that the person from whom the *Vedas* emanated, is in their midst for their sake. They even ask, in their pride, for a few more chances. This has been the case, in all ages. People may be very near (*physically*) to the *Avatar* (Divine Incarnation), but they live out their lives, unaware of their fortune, they exaggerate the role of *Miracles*, which are as trivial when compared to *My Glory* and *My Majesty*, as a mosquito in size and strength to the elephant upon which it squats. Therefore, when you speak about these *Miracles,* I smile within Myself out of pity that you allow yourself so easily, to lose the precious awareness of My Reality.

MY VISITING CARD

My power is immeasurable. My Truth is inexplicable. I am announcing this about Me, for the need has arisen, but what I am doing now, is only the gift of a '*visiting card!*' Let me tell you that emphatic declarations of the truth by *Avatars*, were made so clearly, and so un-mistakably, only by *Krishna.* In spite of the declaration, you will notice in the career of the same *Krishna*, that he underwent defeat in his efforts and endeavors, on a few occasions. You must also note that those defeats too were part of the drama which He had planned, and which He Himself directed. For example, when many kings pleaded with Him to avert the war with the *Kauravas,* He confessed that his peace mission at the *Kauravas Court* had failed, but He had not willed that it should succeed! He had decided that the war would be waged! His Mission was intended to demonstrate the greed and iniquity of the *Kauravas,* and to condemn them before the whole world.

LOVE IS THE ROYAL ROAD THAT
LEADS MANKIND TO GOD

Now, I must tell you, that during the time of this *Sai Avatar*, there is no place for even such drama with scenes of failures and defeats! What I Will must take place, What I Say must succeed. I Am Truth and Truth has no need to hesitate, or fear, or bend. Willing is superfluous for me, for My Grace is ever available to devotees who have steady love and faith. Since I move freely among them, talking and singing, even intellectuals are unable to grasp My Truth, My Power, My Glory, or My Real Task, as *Avatar*. I can solve any problem however knotty. I am beyond the reach of the most intensive enquiry, and the most meticulous measurement. Only those who have recognized My Love, and experienced that Love, can assert that they have glimpsed My Reality, for the path of love is the royal road that leads mankind to Me.

Do not attempt to know Me through the external eyes. When you go to a temple and stand before the image of God, you pray with closed eyes, don't you? Why? Because you feel that the inner eye of wisdom alone can reveal Him to you. Therefore, do not crave from Me trivial material objects, but crave for Me, and you would be rewarded. Not that you should not receive whatever objects I give as a sign of grace out of the fullness of Love. I shall tell you why I give these rings, talismans, rosaries etc. It is to signify the bond between Me and those to whom they are given. When calamity befalls them, the article comes to me in a flash, taking from Me the remedial grace of protection. That Grace is available to all who call on Me, in any Name or Form, not merely to those who wear these gifts. Love is the bond that wins Grace.

BHAGAVAN SATHYA SAI BABA IS THE
DIVINE MOTHER AND FATHER

Understand the meaning of the Name *Sai Baba. 'Sa'* means *Divine, 'Ai' or 'Ayi'* means *'Mother'* and *'Baba'* means *'Father'.* The Name indicates the Divine Mother and Father, just as *'Samba Siva',* which also means the *Divine Mother* and *Father.* Your physical parents exhibit love with a dose of selfishness, but this *Sai (Mother and Father)* showers affection, or reprimands, only to lead you towards victory in the struggle for Self-Realization.

LOVE IS MY INSTRUMENT

I have come, in order to achieve the supreme task of uniting as One family, the entire of mankind, through the bond of brotherhood; of affirming and illumining the *Atmic Reality* of each being, in order to reveal God, which is the basis on which the entire Cosmos rests; and of instructing all to recognize the common divine heritage that binds man to man, so that man can rid himself of his animal nature, and rise into the divinity which is his goal.

I Am the Embodiment of Love. Love is My instrument. There is no creature without Love, even the least fortunate loves himself at least, and his soul is God. So, there are no atheists, though some might dislike Him or refuse Him, as malarial patients dislike sweets, or diabetic patients refuse to have anything to do with sweets! Those who preen themselves as atheists will one day, when their illness is gone, relish God and revere Him.

I need to tell you so much about My Truth, for I desire that you should contemplate on this and derive joy therefrom, so that you may be inspired to observe the disciplines laid down, and progress towards the goal of Self-realization, the realization of the *Sai* that shines in your heart.

God has in His Hand, the string of the kite which is man. Sometimes He may give it a pull, sometimes He may loosen the hold, but whatever He Does, be confident and carefree, for it is He alone, that holds the string. That faith ever present, that feeling hardening into a *Samskara*, will fill you with *Premarasa* (a fountain of love).

MY REALITY

I must tell you one fact. World conferences dedicated to religion or spiritual problems have been held in the past, as have conferences of the followers of these same faiths, but these have been held only after the decease of the founders, or divine inspirers. This is the very first time that a world conference is being held while the Incarnation is present before everyone, with the body assumed for the purpose of Incarnation, and the name *Sathya* chosen by him, for Himself.

Ninety-nine out of a hundred of you do not strive to know My Reality. You cannot understand My Reality, either today, or even after thousands of years of austerity or enquiry, even if all mankind joins in that effort. But very soon, you will be aware of My Glory offered by the Divine Principle, which has taken upon Itself, this body and this name. Your good fortune, therefore, is greater than that which was the share of sages and saints, and even personalities who have incarnated different aspects of this Divine Glory. Since I move about with you, eat with you, and talk to you, you are deluded into a belief that it is but an instance of common humanity. Be warned against this mistake. I am also deluding you by My Talking with you, engaging Myself in activities with you, but in any moment, My Divinity may reveal Itself to you. You must be ready, prepared for that moment. When God is incarnated in human form, you must endeavor to overcome *Maya* (delusion) that hides it from your eyes.

BHAGAVAN SRI SATHYA SAI BABA –
THE INCARNATION OF ALL FORMS OF GOD

This is a human form in which every divine entity, every divine principle, that is to say, all Names and Forms ascribed by Man to God are manifest. Do not allow doubt to distract you. If you only install in the altar of your heart, steady faith in My Reality as *Sarva-Daivathwaswarupam*, (the incarnation of all the forms of God) you can soon have a vision of My Reality. If instead, you swing back and forth, like the pendulum of a clock, you can never succeed in comprehending the truth and winning that bliss.

Let me draw your attention to another fact. In spite of plenty of patent evidence of His Grace, on previous occasions when God was incarnated on earth, the bliss of recognizing Him as a Divine Incarnation was only accorded to a few people, until the physical embodiment had left the world. The loyalty and devotion such divine personages formerly commanded from men, arose through fear and awe at their superhuman powers and skills, or at their imperial and penal authority. But ponder a moment at this *Sathya Sai* manifestation! In this age of rampant materialism, aggressive disbelief, and irreverence, what is it that draws to itself the adoration of millions from all over the world? It is supra-world Divinity in human Form

THE SAI SANKALPAM

How blessed you are, that you can witness all the countries of the world paying tribute to *Bharath* (India). You can also hear adoration to the name *Sathya Sai* reverberating throughout the World, even while this body is before you, not at some future date when he has left the world. You can also equally witness another fact. I will restore *Dharma* to its true and natural state. The *Sanathana*

Dharma laid down in the *Vedas,* for the good of all people of the world, is the eternal principle for the *moral* righteousness of society.

> ***"I Will Sustain Truth – I Will Uproot Un-Truth.***
> ***I Will Make All of You Exult on that Victory***
> ***and that Achievement.***
> ***That is the Sai Sankalpa"***

Bhagavan Sri Sathya Sai Baba Declaration at the World Conference, Bombay May 17[th]1968

Bhagwan Sri Sathya Sai BABA'S 67th Birthday
Celebration at Hill view Stadium on 22nd / 23rd Nov. 1992

17

VISION OF GOD

You are, I know, rather bored by these evening gatherings taking place every day without break, for it is hard listening to the discussion of spiritual subjects, and the detailing of disciplinary rules. Some of you are saying that you came to *Prasanthi Nilayam* for peace and quiet, but you are being subjected to the ordeal of long speeches sitting in conferences. Let Me tell you that discourses by these great scholars are very valuable. The speakers here are blessed, as are the listeners. In fact, the listeners are even more blessed, for they can very often follow the lessons which these speakers teach, while the teachers themselves might not be able to carry them out.

SING THE NAME OF RAMA

There was a *Pandith* who led a disciplined life, sticking to a pre-arranged timetable. He woke up from sleep in the early hours of the morning, recited the *Pranava* (Om), and later, after ablutions, drank his cup of milk at 7am exactly. Some days the milkmaid arrived late, for she lived on the other bank of the river and had to catch a ferry to cross over with the milk. The ferry boat either started a little too soon, or at times reached her bank too late, when she then brought the milk late, to the great annoyance of the *Pandith*. One day, he lost patience and chastised her for upsetting his timetable:

> "*Why do you depend on that horrid boat to take you across? Do you not know that if you only repeat the name of Rama, that you can walk across without coming to harm? Rama will see that you do not get drowned.*"

Next day, the maid repeated the name of *Rama*, and calmly crossed the river. Yes, her faith gave her the strength. She did not tarry for the ferry. The *Pandith* was flabbergasted, for he did not believe that it could ever be possible, that by just saying the name of *Rama,* such a miracle could work. The *bhaktha* must ignore his identity and separateness and merge with the Ideal. What individuality has the servant got? He has nothing, no, not even a trace. The Master is All.

THE SADHA-SHIVALINGAM –
THE CARDINAL VISION OF UNITY

If you stare at the sun for a second, and then turn your eye to other things around, you will find that there is a dark patch over them, and you cannot recognize them. Similarly, once you get a vision of the *Purusha* (*God*), who is more effulgent than a thousand suns, you can no longer recognize the multiplicity called *Prakriti* (*Nature*). The world appears black to you, it is blocked, indeed you can no longer recognize or deal with variety, once you have had a vision of the basic unity. Take the screen in the cinema theatre. When the film is on, you do not see the screen, you see only the play. When the show is over, you see just a screen, a screen that has no message – neither voice, nor name, nor color, nor creed. That is *Brahman.* Very often an entire rope gives the appearance of a snake in the dark. In this previous example, the entire screen disappears into the image in the picture. *Brahman* is *Sathyam; Jagath* (Universe) is *Brahman.* That is *Sath* (Being), this is *Chith* (Awareness). Knowing this and dealing with both is *Anandham* (Bliss). I was asked once how anyone can accept the two seemingly opposite statements:*'Brahma Sathyam Jaganmithya,* and *Sarvam Vishnumayam Jagath'* – *Brahman* is God, world is false, and world is full of *Vishnu.*

This was My reply: The powers of man are limited by his experience and his knowledge. He is only a *Pinda* (part), while the Lord is *Anda* (whole), the force pervading the entire universe. The *Anda-Pinda Lingam* symbolizes this body-mind relationship, which arises from an aspect of God (*Madhava*).

The *Sadha Shivalingam* represents the ever-auspicious *Atma,* which is beyond all dual aspects and concepts, immanent in all beings, and everywhere. It is not subject to time, it is Sadha-Shivam: *Sadha* (always), *Shivam* (beneficial and auspicious).

THE TRUE MASTER IS ALWAYS HAPPY

The *Jnanalingam* is the sign of the attainment of *Jnana* (spiritual wisdom), when the last vestige of the delusion of 'I" is wiped off, even the feeling '*I Know*' is gone; then you are the *Atma,* pure and whole, entire, and enduring, then your condition is best represented by the *Athmalinga.*

Each one of you possesses the tremendous *Shakthi* (power) of the *Atma* (infinite consciousness) in you. Some are able to draw upon it, others just know it is there; others are unaware of the methods of tapping it, or even of its existence, however it all comes in time through steady discipline (sadhana). The child, in time becomes the father; the father becomes a grandfather. The *Sadhaka* advances step by step to the ultimate bliss by adhering to the instructions of the *Guru*.

You should tell the *Guru "If you can help me, do so. If you cannot, do not give false hopes and mislead me into false ways. Confess your immaturity. I can then seek some other guide. Do not pretend to be a teacher, when you are not even a good student"* Ply him with questions, examine his daily conduct, clear your doubts, then cultivate faith in the *Guru* you have chosen. There are many *Gurus* who are guided by their students and their followers and warned by their disciples not to state certain views in public. These *Gurus* act according to the dictates of men in power, and men with money. A real *Guru* must be like *Sadha-Shivalingam*, full of *Anandha* welling up from the consciousness of God.

NEVER DENY YOUR TRUE NATURE

So long as you are in *Avidhya* (*ignorance*), so long as you are untrained and lacking in knowledge, you cannot experience bliss; you cannot attain it. You are still bound by the three-corded rope – The black cord of *Thamas* (inertia), the red cord of *Rajas* (passion), and the white cord of *Sathwa* (equanimity). Deny that you are bound, and the rope will disappear. Hence regulate your life in such a way that you do not harm your inner nature. That is to say, live in the constant contemplation of your kindred with others and with God. Do good to others, treat all nature kindly, speak soft and sweet, become a child devoid of envy, hate and greed. When your ego crosses the threshold of your family and sets out to love others in brotherhood, you have taken the first steps to cross the threshold of *Maya*. Whoever has tasted that

Joy, will thence forward crave for that only. How can the *Jeevi* (individual being) stoop to anything less? How can the truth be grasped when you are steeped in Falsehood? How can a fish experience the sky? How can nectar and poison, day and night, God and the Devil, be together?

SEE SHIVA IN EVERYONE AND IN EVERYTHING

Uddhava, when he came among the *Gopi's*, discovered that *Krishna* was permanently present in their hearts. They were seen scanning the dust on the roads to discover footprints of *Krishna*, so that they could fall down, and worship it! *Radha* was the greatest devotee of all. She saw all footprints as *Krishna's* own, including even Hers. Ultimately, is there anyone who is not him, any form that is not His, any name that does not belong to Him! *Uddhava* exclaimed *"I have no need of Narayana; I am content with this vision of the Glory of the bhaktha"*. The same prescription also holds for the sorrow and fear of today. See Him in all as the *Shiva-Swarupa* (form of *Shiva*); then all will yield joy and peace. That is the Truth. The rest is False. *Yama* (the God of Death) comes with delusion. *Shiva* is seen when the light dawns.

LOVE DESTROYS THE ROOTS OF EGO

Ahamkara, or Egotism, is *Maya.* How can you get rid of it? The field looks a dry waste, with no sign of green, and you feel proud that you have pulled up all the grass by the roots. When the showers come down, they sprout again. *Prema* (love) will destroy the roots of the ego. Plant it, protect it, foster it, and enjoy its fruits. Remove envy, haste, and greed from your heart. They will smother the seedlings of *Prema* (Love).

HAVE FAITH FIRST

Have faith. Faith will grant you all that you need. How can you build your faith on a mound of sand? The deeper you dig the sandy soil, the greater the risk for the sides slipping down and burying your faith in doubt and denial. Listen to the call from within. Believe that it is the call from *Mathura* (birthplace of *Krishna*).

The Lord Himself condescends to grant you the opportunity to develop faith. Why did *Krishna* raise the *Govardhana Hill* and keep it aloft? It was to announce His Truth, and His Nature, to instill faith, and to implant courage. It is just a sign, as is each one of My Acts. There is no task which I cannot accomplish, remember; there is no weight I cannot lift. You have faith in *Rama* and *Krishna,* because of books which describe a part of their achievements, and the experience of the *Sadhakas* who attempted to delve into their mystery. You have not demanded direct proof of divinity from either *Rama* or *Krishna*, have you? Have faith first and then you will get proof enough.

Take up the discipline of the repetition of God's Name. Why drag out your existence as a mere consumer of food, as a moving burden encumbering the earth? Eat, but transform food into good deeds, good thoughts, and sweet speech. Move, but do not cause pain to others, or add to their misery. Do not condemn yourselves as weak, sinful, conceited, wicked, outlawed, mean etc. When you so condemn yourself, remember that you are also condemning Me, who is your Inner Self. Live, so that with every breath and step, you come nearer and nearer to Me.

Bhagavan Sri Sathya Sai Discourse
Prasanthi Nilayam, October 22ⁿᵈ, 1961.

'Upavasa, means that all your thoughts, deeds, and words, on those holy days must be about God, that you should spend the day: 'Near Him, 'In Him, and 'For Him. It means that eating, sleeping and other bodily activities have to take a secondary role and that meditation, and Japam – must take the main role.

Sathya Sai Baba

18

MY OMNIPRESENCE

Bhadram, has pleased you all by his *Kathakalashhepam* (musical discourse on mythological stories of *India*). He was worried that he was in indifferent health, but enthusiasm overcame physical weakness. Devotion gave the required energy. His emotions were riding the clouds of exultation; His voice, however, was creeping along the marshlands of convalescence. You also, went through the ordeal of squatting on the floor for over two hours. That is the true spirit, not to attach undue importance to the temporary complaints of the body. The long and the short of the *Katha* (story) which *Bhadram* recited and commented upon is this: The Lord is *Natanasuthradhari* (he who pulls the strings in the play of puppetry). It looks as if the dolls dance of their own accord and play out a plot of their own, that there is no one behind the drama to direct it, that the dolls are alive and full of activity. The strings are invisible to you. It is the mind that deceives you thus.

I AM THE ETERNAL WITNESS

Baba here sang a song: One man's mind prefers *Krishna,* another likes *Shiva,* another prefers the formless *Allah.* He said "My voice, you have noted gets lost exactly here, because in the song the next line is about some preferring the name of *Sai.* I never call upon people to worship Me, giving up the forms they already revere. I have come to establish *Dharma,* and so I do not, and will not, demand or require your homage. Give it to your Lord or *Guru,* whoever He Is. I am the Eternal Witness, come to set right the Vision"

PURIFY YOUR MIND BY MORAL CONDUCT

In the *Katha* (stories) *Bhadram* referred to *Krishna* and His deeds, how he killed His maternal uncle etc. but all that was in His Plan, part of the Divine task. When the truth demands fulfilment, no flimsy physical bond can stand in the way. The Lord cares only for the devotion of those whose heart belongs to Him. He cares for *bhakthi,* not *bhakthas.* He will not be partial to worldly family bonds, nor swayed by any such affiliations. Those reciters and exponents who have lowered the *Leelas* (divine plays) of the Lord, trying to please the common folk, made *Narada* a crook of low intrigue, *Vishwamitra* a fool, *Hanuman* a monkey, and *Rama* a mere man. They create the impression that God is jealous, greedy, vengeful, and subject to human passions. They seldom reveal stories, or incidents, the names, forms, and realities of the personalities of the *Puranas* (sacred texts), the deep hidden meanings, nor the symbolism of the texts. They should interpret the incidents with reference to the context of spiritual progress. They should judge actions with reference to the standards of the age in which they happened, not by placing them against the background of modern times. People should be transformed by these discourses: they should have the effect on those people like the thrill of a bath in the sacred waters of the holy *Ganga*. The narrator himself must strive to live this spiritual experience, by the sincere discipline of his own *Sadhana*. That alone can give pro- found satisfaction to the listeners, not his imagining the authentic joy he himself can experience

Of course, if you still have doubts, you must purify your mind in adopting a moral code of conduct and a constant spiritual discipline. Then the truth will be reflected more and more clearly in your mind. As this process is continued, the tendencies of all worldly desires must be eliminated. They must fade and fall, as the petals of a flower grow old. They should not be plucked and cast aside. The noise of the marketplace should give place to the silence of the altar, only then can the secret whisper of the conscience be heard, and the warning signal of the *Sasthras,* be recognized.

NOTHING CAN HAPPEN WITHOUT GOD'S WILL

Athmashakthi (The power of the soul) can only function when activated by *Mayashakthi* (The power of illusion). That is why *Maya* (the cosmic illusion) *or the Cosmos,* was born just before *Krishna*. If *Maya* did not exist, how could the drama take place? In reality, it is therefore *Maya* (the grand illusion) who announces the arrival of these personages and their identities. *Ashanti* (The absence of peace) i.e. your physical and mental suffering, and everything of that kind that troubles naturally and completely, irresistibly brings you to Me. Having arrived at my feet, try not to concentrate on the material gifts which you can receive from me. Above all, you should accept My precious advice for your spiritual progress. You should also pray like this:

O Lord,
Asatho Maa Sad Gamaya
Thamaso Maa Jyothir Gamaya
Mrityor Maa, Amritham Gamaya
Om Shanti, Shanti, Shanti.

From Falsehood Lead me to Truth,
From Darkness Lead me to Light,
From Death, lead me to immortality,
Om, Peace, Peace, Peace.

Is there any end to the list of worldly pleasures that you crave for? Have you not noticed that when you acquire one, another starts tantalizing you? If you do not obtain what you want, very often, your link with God also loosens. If you lose something, or if something is lost or stolen from you, you lose faith in me. I have not come to guard your jewels and your 'valuables'. I have come to guard your virtue and holiness, and to guide you to the ultimate goal.

If your goodness is in danger, come to Me, and I will show you how to develop it and make it blossom. If someone is snatched away by death, while on pilgrimage to *Khasi* or *Badrinath*, you quickly console yourself that it was an enviable death. But if you get even a mild headache at *Puttaparthi*, you start blaming Me. According to you, those who have entered this compound once should not die. If they do, your faith wavers and diminishes. Well, not even an eyelid can open without God's will. So, try to get God's Grace, and leave the answers to all your questions, according to His Will.

MY FEET ARE ALWAYS WITHIN YOUR REACH

When the sun rises on the lake, all the buds of the lotus will not open out in full bloom. Only those which are full grown can blossom, the rest must patiently await their turn. Everyone has the right to God's Grace, but it can be won only by a constant spiritual discipline alone. There is no trace of anger or hatred in Me. My life blood is *Prema* (love), and I am the Source of *Dhaya* (compassion). Try to understand Me and to know My True Nature. The reflection of the Moon in the depths of the lake seems to quiver and shake because of the waves, but raise your head a little and look up, and you can see the moon is steady as ever.

I Am also, always unshakeable and My Grace is Omnipresent. To the outward eye, My Action appears magical, miraculous; but to the inner eye, it is all simply *Divine Leela* (Divine Play). In fact, the hand that creates, is also the same which gives, – nothing is withheld. It is always for you and you alone that this hand acts. This is My Truth; This is My Reality. Know this and be happy. I have started the work for which I have come. I have collected the metal, the steel, the stones, the bricks. I have dug the foundations, and soon the superstructure will take shape. Nothing can stop this. You will see with your own eyes, thousands rushing towards the gates of *Nilayam* and hundreds of thousands on every rock of the surrounding hills. The *bhakthas* who are permanently at *Nilayam,* are sad that they have had no chance of even a *Namaskaram* (respectful obeisance) for three months. They feel that those who come from afar, and leave in a few days, have a greater chance, as I specifically accord this privilege to them. To them, I say this "You are deluded by a false sense of values. Why worry so much at not being able to touch these feet? My feet are within your reach at all times, wherever you are. '*Sarvathah Pani Padhah – Hands and Feet everywhere'*

If you wail in agony "*Don't you hear me?*" My ears are there to listen. If you pray from the depths of your heart" *Don't you see my plight?"* My eyes are there showering Grace on you. Once and for all, escape from this *Maya,* (the illusion that this world is real) and become *Prema (love)*. Only then, will you receive *Prema* (love) from Me.

PUTTAPARTHI WILL BECOME MATHURA NAGARA

Rama, Krishna, and *Sai Baba* appear differently because of the dress each has donned, but it is the same divine entity, believe Me. Do not allow yourself to be misled and don't get lost. The time is soon approaching when this huge building, or even vaster ones, will be too small for the gatherings of those who are called to this place. In the future, the sky itself, will be the roof of the auditorium. I will forego the car and even the airplane, when I move from place to place, for the crowds pressing around them will be too huge. I will have to move across the sky; Yes, you will see, this also shall happen, believe Me.

You will witness *Puttaparthi* becoming *Mathura Nagara* (birthplace of *Krishna*). No one in the world can stop this development or delay it.

I will not give you up, and I will not allow anyone abandon Me. Even if you lose faith, you will repent, and quickly return to this refuge, loudly clamouring for readmission. I shall be in this body for 58 years more. I have assured you of this already. Your lives are intertwined with My Worldly Mission. Do everything in accordance with this great privilege.

Bhagavan Sri Sathya Sai Divine Discourse
Prasanthi Nilayam, October 21st, 1961.

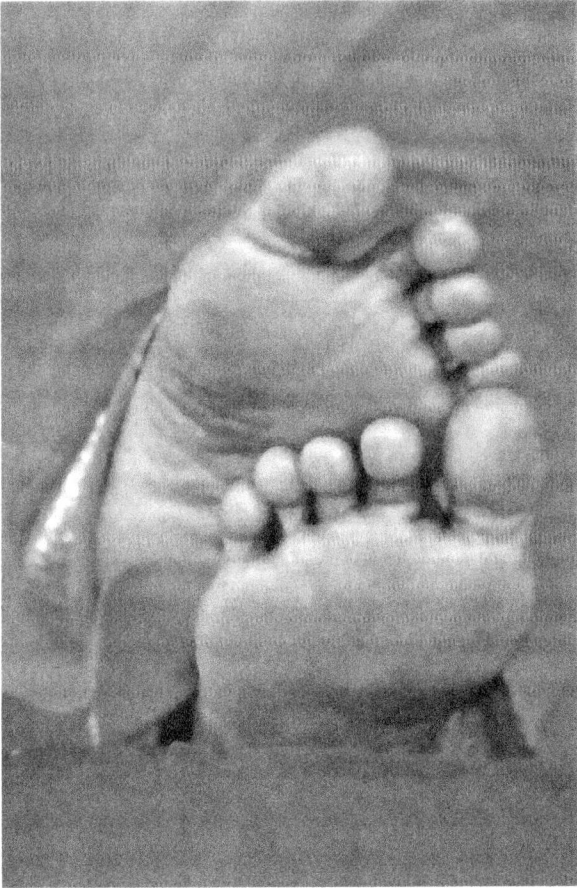

My Feet Are Always Within Your Reach,
At Any Time Wherever You Are.

19

SEE GOD IN ALL

Yesterday, and the day before, I spoke about the disciplinary life that you should lead. I was a harsh taskmaster, but today, I shall be soft, and My Words will be like the Himalayan breeze, cool and invigorating. That harshness had a reason, for there can be no effect without a cause. This coolness and that warmth are both parts of the same person, and you cannot accept the one and reject the other. Good and bad, right and wrong, are two sides of the same coin.

ONLY THE ATMA-SOUL HAS
AUTHORITY TO COMMAND

As for Me, My Nature is distinct. I do not identify with anything. Those who have neither authority nor adeptness, have to hear, study, analyze, and judge. Authority is the right of the *Atma* alone. It is the *Atma* that can command. For Me, the purity of

139

your feeling is important, not the depth of your scholarship. That is why I was harsh yesterday and the day before, to compel you to examine your feelings and remove the blemishes. Today, I assure you, I shall not be harsh. In fact, you may have noticed, I used the word, *Premaswarupulara* (Embodiments of Divine Love), in the beginning when I began to speak. Today man generally attaches more importance to intellectual acuity than to emotional clarity, but that's an incomplete analysis. Emotional clarity is as important as intellectual acuity. Your emotions serve you every day, and they influence your habits, without your even noticing. When you buy an article from a shop, you don't just see its practical use, but you also allow yourself to be seduced by its external packaging, is that not so? That's to say the object provokes an emotional reaction in you as well as an intellectual one. *Bhava* (the good feeling or internal predisposition) attributes beauty (*Andham*) to objects' That is why I often say, *Andham is Anandham* (beauty is bliss); you cannot have one without the other.

GAIN THE EXPERIENCE OF UNITY

Andham, and *Anandham,* (beauty, harmony, and ecstasy) are found in *Ekathwam* (Oneness), the discovery and experience of unity. Oneness must be understood by the experience of the union of different elements, for example gold and mud, or by the experience of Oneness, through *bhava* (the merging of *the sight*, the *object se*en, and the *subjective seer*). These are the three elements of your quest. If you grasp this, your success is guaranteed. *Ramakrishna,* (*the great Hindu saint*) was motivated by this ardent desire. He promoted this same hunger for truth in *Vivekananda,* and in all others who came to him. You too, must try with all your might, to gain your own experience and to grasp this success with the yearning (*Bhava*) of your soul, to also earn and enjoy the fruits of your efforts. This is the essence of his teaching.

The music of all the transmitters of the world vibrates everywhere, but if you truly want to hear it, you need to have a good radio, turn it on, and tune it to the right frequency. Likewise, the key to liberation has to be cast, forged, filed, and adapted for each individual. It doesn't fall from the sky! *Ramakrishna* Himself sought for it through years of inexplicable anguish. Why should God shorten this process for anyone else? No one can come to you saying: *"Here it is"* Each flower needs to yield its fruit, and the fruit has to grow, ripen and detach from the branch.

Jealousy and anger are the twins born of the mother *Ahamkara* (Ego), the sense of possessiveness. Destroy these two twins of jealousy and anger and take the *Karam* (meaning in Telugu 'the spicy taste' of the *Ahamkaram*), and simply keep the *Aham* (*the I*) so with this tool you can get the gentle thrill of *Aham Brahmasmi* (I am Brahman . . . I am God). That is the mountain to be scaled, the goal to be attained. The *Karam* in the *Aham*, as in the *Ahamkaram* (ego) is like the single seed, which if allowed to germinate multiplies a thousand-fold and produces many bags of seeds. It has to be crushed in the very first instance. Then, the analysis of the *Aham,* starts and ends in this conclusion: *Ayam Athma Brahma.* This *Aham* is the *Athma,* the Universal Soul which is *Brahma.* These two expressions: *Thath and Thwam* (That and This) are identified, and 'This' is found to be none other than 'That', when *Thath Thwam Asi* (Thou Art That) is realized. So, what is this thing called *Thath*? What is *Brahman*? In other words? What Is God? *Mahavakya* (The Fourth Great Revelation) declares: 'He is *Prajnanam* – Unity, One without Other.

SACRED TRUTHS REVEALED
THE FOUR MAHAVAKYAS

All these *Mahavakyas* (sacred statements of supreme truth), describes this unique Entity and His Glory without equal, as an Ocean of Grace. The water vapor arising from it is *Prajnanam Brahma* (the highest wisdom). The cloud which forms is *Ayam Athma Brahma* (I am the soul). The shower of rain which results is *Thath Thwam Asi* (Thou art that), and the river is *Aham Brahmasmi* – I am *Brahman*. (I am God). *Prajnanam Brahma* (the highest wisdom) is symbolized by *Anda-Pinda Lingam* (The Cosmic Lingam) – The Vision of the One and the same entity through all the manifold different entities. This is the expansion of the individual into the universal, the merging of the '*I*' into the vastness of the 'He' and "We'.

When you knock at a door and someone inside answers you with the question: *"Who is it?"* you automatically answer: *"It's Me"*. That does not satisfy the questioner, so another question eliciting further information follows to determine your identity before the door will be opened. The same is true for the door of liberation. It doesn't open except to the people who can give the correct answer, which is "I Am God"

SADHASHIVA LINGAM –
THE VISION OF THE ETERNAL SHIVA

This vision helps the *Jeeva* (individual soul), to realize above all '*I am in the Light*'. The second *Mahavakya,* reveals to him *Ayam Athma Brahma*, (*The Light is in me*). Slowly the truth illuminates the spirit! The light which I imagined as enveloping me, the *Prajnanam,* which I identified as the basis of all appearances, that illumination is in me too. My true reality is also that *Prajnanam,* that *Light*. This is represented *by Sadha-Shiva Lingam* – (The vision of the eternal *Shiva*).

PERSONAL EXPERIENCE IS
THE BEST TEACHER

Because of his discipline, the *Sadhaka* experiences the light which dispels the darkness accumulated from his past lives. He realizes that he is that light, and nothing else.

He then becomes immune to spasms of ignorance which make him forget his nature, just as a beginner learning the violin lapses easily into grinding out discordant notes of discontent and grief. The devotee also sometimes expresses discontent and sorrow. When the pain becomes unbearable, the person who is suffering, faints, and loses consciousness, which could be a consolation. Beyond a certain limit God will not allow suffering. Similarly, when this Divine identity is established, no more activity is possible. One becomes unconscious of the world, or more precisely, one passes beyond the realms of consciousness; – unconsciousness, subconsciousness, and even super consciousness. The river has at last reached the Ocean. *Thath Thwam Asi* – You Are That. This state is symbolized by *the Jnana Linga* (illumination by experience)

Aham Brahmasmi – the last of the *Mahavakyas,* is symbolised by the *Athma-Lingam.* The fourteen higher worlds, and the fourteen lower worlds are beyond description. They are symbolic of the different levels of consciousness in the geography of the Soul, on the long journey towards the final destination. There are no books that can teach you the topography. The journey is the best teacher, each step making the next one easier. The greatest devotees of The Lord, *Radha, Mira, Suku, Surdas, Ramakrishna* – all followed the guidance of their own inner voice to arrive at the goal.

The *Angam* (*body*) is the *Sangam* (meeting point) where spirit and matter meet; the *Jangam*, the moving phantasmagoria where spirit and matter meet, is in *Sangam.* From this *Sangam*, one has to evoke the *Lingam* (divinity) in its aforesaid four forms, one after the other. The *Lingam* is just a sign, a sign of endeavor, a sign of success. For example, the *Anda Pinda Lingam* signifies the egg-shaped universe, which is how it is, even according to experts in science. The outer cover is the *Anda,* and the inner *Rasa* or matter is the *Pinda.* They are both dependent, one on the other. You are all basically the *Anda Pinda*, with the outer shell of materialism and the inner core of divinity. The body is a vessel to contain the *Chaitanya,* i.e. the effulgence of God

ATMA-LINGAM IS THE ULTIMATE PHASE

The idea of being Brahman (*Aham Brahmasmi*) revealed in the *Mahavakya,* creates a link of kinship; and that sense of belonging has great spiritual comfort. This attachment ultimately creates a fusional state between you and God. For example, when your own child cries, you are more anxious than when it is the child of another, is that not true? This attachment is the root cause of your anxiety. Similarly, the Supreme God temporarily incarnates in response to the cry of his children. In fact, God is also *Anda Pindam* when he comes with human body or as materialized form, whether that form be *Maha Vishnu, Shiva, Rama, Krishna* or *Sathya Sai Baba. Jnanalingam* symbolizes wisdom, the innate knowledge born from spiritual awareness which reveals that you are *Sarvabhutha* (the reality and totality of all beings) and that this reality (*Sarvabhutha*) is in you. The *Jnanam* (divine wisdom) is *God, Brahma* himself. *Jnana* is not a quality of *Brahman;* it is *Brahman* Itself, for *Brahman* has no quality. The *Jnani* (the liberated person), though in the world, has the inner vision which makes him fall away from the twig as the dried leaf, which has no more need of attachment to the branch.

Athmalingam (the vision of the Self), the ultimate phase, corresponds to the state of Gold, from which all the names and forms of golden jewels have melded. Just as cold-water freezes into ice; one can also say that the soul (*Atma*), freezes and becomes the individual, specific form. The *Atmalingam,* is not the story of the vase which contains seawater, it is itself immersed in the same ocean. Both are identical, only the name and the form are different.

You can realize your truth by following the path which will lead to that knowledge, only you must be prepared to submerge yourself in discipline and work seriously. When I give you a medicine, you must take it in the prescribed dosage, and adhere strictly to the regimen of food, sleep and exercise I recommend. Of course, the anxiety to get cured quickly is commendable, but there is a timetable for all of this. Moderation is much more efficient than excess. When cooking a sauce, women know, that as well as adding water to reduce the taste of too much salt, they also have to add the necessary quantities of other ingredients to make it tasty. In the same way, I must reduce the excessive attachment you have for the things of the world, and little by little, I have to correct by using various different methods.

I will cure you slowly and patiently. The more slowly I do it, the more lasting it will be. I shall reveal to you the *Atmalingam* have no doubt! Yes, great days are coming. Do not deprive yourself of this chance because of your laziness. When you listen to the story of My Life, you finish by forgetting the story of the world, and live only in My Story, until there is no separate story for you to relate to, or live. My story is a pretext to make you forget all other stories.

INSTALL SADHA-SHIVALINGAM IN YOUR HEART

Sadha-Shivalingam indicates the person who was, is, and will be, for all time the form of *Shiva* (*Swarupa*). Here and everywhere, night and day, in joy and grief, he is *Shivam*; that is to say, always happy, auspicious, and full of grace. *Anandham* (bliss) is his breath, his motivating force, his state, his expression, are all pure Grace. His nature is always perfect happiness. There is no room here for controversy, intellectual rivalry, nor any competition of the *Pandith's* and scholars, wasting the valuable paper manufactured by the mills of this country. Step by step, by the Grace of the Divinity which resides in you, install *Sadha-Shivalingam* in your consciousness, and all things will be revealed to you.

Bhagavan Sri Sathya Sai Baba Divine Discourse
Prasanthi Nilayam October 20th, 1961

20

HUMAN DESTINY

Most people in the world do not know the true significance of life. Many do not even seem to care about it. One in a million may be concerned about knowing the purpose of life. This concern is the first step in the long journey which leads towards the ultimate goal. Most young people are content to regard eating, sleeping, dressing, and rearing a big family as the principle aims of living. No doubt all these are necessary up to a certain point, but these objectives alone cannot contribute to inner peace, or a life of fulfilment.

The phenomena of the external world are what the eyes see, the ears hear, and what the mind perceives. All these are sensory phenomena. Beyond the senses (*Indriyas*), is the mind, and greater than the mind, is the intellect (*Buddhi*). The intellect is governed by the soul (*Atma.*)

HUMAN DESTINY IS TO REALISE
THE SOUL-ATMA

Among the sensory organs, the most powerful is the mouth (which has the powers of speech and consuming food). When the mouth is under the control of the mind, all other senses can be controlled. Speech must be restrained as much as possible, then the attention of the mind must be directed towards the intellect (*Buddhi*) which has the power of discrimination. When the *Buddhi* is turned towards the *Atma* (the indwelling Spirit), it begins to realize the Omnipresent God.

THE BLISS OF THE SPIRIT

The inextricable connection between the material world and the internal world of consciousness, eludes the understanding of ordinary people. They are plunged into the desire of enjoying worldly pleasures, and they do not attempt to discover the unlimited joy to be derived from the inner spirit. This is because all the sense organs are only oriented to experiences from the outside. It is not surprising that the common man is subject to the outward vision. Only very few develop the inner vision and enjoy spiritual bliss. Is it the body that derives joy from looking at a thing of beauty, or is it the *Atma*? What is it that relishes the food that is consumed – the body or the spirit? What is it that enjoys fragrance, or is moved by companionship? Inquiring in this manner, it will be found that the body is, a gross mass, incapable of experiencing joy. It is the *Atma* that is the enjoyer, and not the physical body. It must be realized that the spirit transcends the mind and the intellect and pervades the entire Cosmos. The spirit is the basis for the awareness of the external world and for experiencing the inner world.

SUPREME CONSCIOUSNESS – PARA VIDYA

The Vedas and Vedangas, (music and literature, physics and chemistry, botany and biology) – all these different branches of knowledge are related to the phenomenal universe. They belong to the category of *Apara Vidya* – (inferior knowledge). People essentially devote their entire lives to studying this knowledge. Only knowledge of the Spirit is Para Vidya – (The Supreme Knowledge). *Apara Vidya* (worldly knowledge) essentially exists for earning a living, but even worldly knowledge serves to point the way to the revelation of spiritual awareness. Without spiritual knowledge, all other knowledge is without value.

Every man must inquire every moment of the purpose and goal of life. Eating, drinking, sleeping, and passing time, cannot be the meaning of human life! All these are common to birds and beasts. What is the unique characteristic of mankind? He is endowed with faculties which can enable him to rise above the state of animal, to that of a human, and then from human to Divine.

THE DIFFERENT LEVELS OF CONSCIOUSNESS

Vaak (Speech), *Manas* (Mind,) and *Prana* (Vital Breath), are manifestations of the Soul (*Atma*). Each is related to a state of consciousness. They are.

1. *Jagrati* (*the waking state*),
2. *Swapna* (*dream state*), and
3. *Sushupti* (*deep sleep state*).

In the *Jagrati state*, man is awake and experiences the outer world through sight, hearing, speech, and other senses. The phenomenal universe is what one experiences through the five sense organs. The experience in the *waking state* is known as *Viswa* (global, total), because the experiences are the subtle form of the Cosmic Principle. *Viswa* has 24 constituent elements: the five organs of action, the five sense organs, the five basic elements, and the five *Pranas* (vital breaths), then the Mind, the *Buddhi* (intellect), the *Chittam* (sub-conscious mind) and the *Ahamkara* (ego-sense). In the dream state, only the four internal senses (the Mind, the Buddhi, the Chitta and the Ahamkara) function. They constitute the *Antahkarana* (the psycho-somatic center). In this state, the individual experiences *Tejas* (the luminous form of consciousness), and is known as *Thaijasa* (higher enlightened being). *Sushupti* is the state of deep sleep. In this state, nothing remains but *Prajna* (the principle of knowing). Hence the experiencer in this state is called *Prajna* (the knower). *Viswa, Thaijasa,* and *Prajna* are all different names of the *Atma* in the different states of consciousness, according to the different forms assumed by the *Atma* in the various states of consciousness.

PRAJNANAM BRAHMA

The *Upanishads* (the sacred texts) *declare: Prajnanam Brahma:* That is to say the different levels of knowledge; *Jnana, Vijnana, Prajnana,* and *Ajnana*, are modifications of one and the same principle of Consciousness. *Prajnana (Consciousness)* is all that is experienced by the *Antahkarana*, through impressions received by the sense organs-the eyes, the ears, the nose, etc. *Prajnana,* is immanent in *Antahkarana,* as the principle which absorbs and interprets the messages received through the senses. The eyes, for instance, are like the bulb in a lamp. The bulb cannot emit light, it needs the electric current to make it burn. Likewise, the eyes cannot see by themselves. It is *Prajnana,* which sees through the eyes. The same thing applies to the ears and other organs. They all need the power of the inner current to do their work. All the sense organs are insentient by themselves. It is *Prajnana* that animates them and makes them instruments of the *Consciousness* (*Chaitanya*).

SAT-CHIT-ANANDA

The Universe contains innumerable objects. In all of them, the one unchanging eternal principle is the *Atma*, that is to say *Prajnana*. This is God (*Brahman*). It is the power of this eternal principle which sustains the evanescent and everchanging objects in the universe. *Asthi, Bhati, and Priyam* are three states of God (Existing, Radiating, and Blessing). *Sat-Chit-Ananda* are the attributes of God. *Sat* indicates Truth, *Chit* indicates Omniscience, *Ananda* is the state of Perfect Bliss. These three attributes of God are changeless and have neither form nor name. When all three are associated with name and form, we obtain the *Prapancha* (the quintuple phenomenal Universe). God permeates throughout the entire Universe. Even if you are unable to see this, God is present in everything. All our senses function because of the Consciousness that operates in every being. Without that Consciousness, man would be an insentient creature

ATMA IS BEYOND THE LIMITS
OF TIME AND SPACE

The different states of consciousness are mutually exclusive. You cannot experience in one state what you have gone through in another state. For instance, in a dream, you might weep for the death of a person, but when you wake up, you don't weep for the person who died in the dream. What happened in the dream is only true in dream state. In the waking state is it unreal (*Mithya*). Likewise, we do not lament in a dream over a person who dies in the waking state. Each experience is real only in its state of consciousness. But the one principle that is common to all the states of consciousness, waking, dream, and deep sleep, is the *Atma*. Atma is not bound by the limitations of time, space, and circumstance.

The body is impermanent, but it is the abode of the Omnipresent spirit. It is a shrine, and when it moves, God moves within it. Hence the body should be cared of in the same way in which an iron safe, which is of little value in itself, is safe-guarded for the sake of the valuables kept within it.

What is it that binds man to the Illusory world? It is neither family nor property. These can be given up when one wishes to do so, but what is most difficult to renounce is *attachment* and *hatred*. If these are dominant in man, he cannot realize his true Self, and if man is unaware of his true Self, he is in bondage. For a man in bondage, there is no freedom from suffering or worry.

THE RIGHTS AND OBLIGATIONS

Students should remember that human life is precious and should not be wasted in the pursuit of trivial and temporary things. Together with academic studies, they should cultivate spiritual *sadhana*. Even in academic studies they should not confine them-selves to merely memorizing what is contained in books. They must digest what they have studied and put their knowledge to practical use in the service of society. Try to absorb what is con-tained in the books and make this knowledge a part of your life. Just as water stored in a reservoir is used for irrigation through canals, the knowledge acquired by you, should be diverted to useful channels for the benefit of society.

Nowadays, everybody talks about their rights and fights for them, but the whole world is forgetting their duties and responsibilities. Rights and duties are like the positive and negative ends of a battery. They go together. When duties are discharged properly, rights will be automatically secured. How can those rights be ensured if the responsibilities are not properly met? Recognize your responsibilities as students. In that way you can earn your rights.

STUDENTS! DEVELOP KIND HEARTEDNESS

This country has inherited a glorious culture from ancient times. You must preserve this culture, while adapting it to suit modern conditions. Most of our students are totally ignorant of our spiritual and cultural heritage. This ancient culture prioritized unity and sought to elevate the human, to divine level. It aimed at promoting religious and social harmony. Today, unity and tolerance are absent, and our society is riddled with conflicts. The country lost its freedom in the past, because of internal divisions. We should regard *Bharat* as one nation, with one heart, and proclaim the truth to the world, with one single voice.

Students! Develop the grandeur of your heart. The heart is not a physical organ. Its name *Hridaya* means the seat of *compassion* (*daya*). Develop compassion for all. Go beyond the narrow mindedness of 'I' and 'Mine' to progress to 'We' and 'Ours'. It is not easy to comprehend the formless, attributeless, infinite Divine. The Truth of God must be discovered and experienced by everyone.

GOD IS OMNIPRESENT

You must lead a life of truth and holiness based on this conviction. Strive to make the nation an upholder of truth and

righteousness. In these times, this is the most important responsibility of students.

*From Bhagavan Sri Sathya Sai's Discourse at the
Sri Sathya Sai Institute Auditorium, Prasanthi
Nilayam, on the Commencement of the
New Academic Year June 22nd, 1987*

21

ATMA-JNANA –
KNOW YOUR SELF

Embodiments of Divine Atma, of all categories of knowledge, the highest is *Atma Jnana* (*the knowledge of the Self*). You may acquire knowledge of the natural sciences, of all arts and crafts, of literature and music, dance and painting, and every conceivable type of worldly knowledge, but none of it will give you peace or bliss, if you do not have knowledge of the Self. Worldly knowledge may bring you fame and prosperity, but only *Atma Jnana* can confer that peace beyond understanding.

Atma Jnana (knowledge of the Self) is that which reveals the unity in diversity, the eternal in the perishable. One who has attained *Atma Jnana,* is Omniscient, (all-knowing). *The Upanishads* say '*Tarata Sokam Atmavith*' (the knower of the Self overcomes sorrow). All worldly knowledge is concerned with sustaining life. When the knowledge of the Soul is acquired, it is then easy to acquire any other kind of knowledge. When communion with God (the Source of all knowledge, power, and wisdom) is established, it is much easier to obtain all knowledge. In fact, through purity of heart and mind, all people should seek to attain Self-Realization.

DEVELOP FAITH IN YOURSELF
AND FAITH IN GOD

Yajnas, and *Yagas,* (acts of charity and virtue, penances, and ceremonial and religious rituals) are all designed to promote purity of heart. Purity of mind is achieved by association with noble personages and studying sacred texts, written by the Saints. The Vedas say, *'Chittasya suddhaye karmah'* Do your duties conscientiously to purify your mind. Purity of mind consciousness leads to realization of the Self. *Atma-Jnana* can be reached only by firm faith. Develop faith in yourself and faith in God. This is the secret of greatness. Self-confidence today is manifest only in matters relating to worldly achievements and self-centered pursuits. In the spiritual domain, faith and confidence are not visibly evident. Without unwavering faith, God cannot be experienced. Because of a lack of firm faith, the formal spiritual practices do not lead to results.

FAITH AND LOVE

The first pre-requisite is an unconditional and unshakeable faith in God. One pointed devotion promotes *shraddha* (spiritual earnestness). The courageous earnest seeker gets knowledge of the Self. The sincere devotee needs no other qualification except deep faith. He needs no other knowledge, no title to lineage or wealth. He may belong to any caste or community. He may be a child, or even an animal like *Gajendra the Lord of the Elephants. Valmiki, Nanda, Kuchela, Dhruva, Gajendra, Sabari, Vidura, and Hanuman* are examples of devotees, who were blessed with

God's Grace through their deep devotion, without any other special qualifications.

To realize God, it is not necessary to have wealth, gold, or other emblems of affluence, nor is great scholarship necessary. All that is needed is pure, selfless devotion without ego. Today, men attempt to worship God, with their egoistic and impure minds. Without purity of thought, speech, and action, it is impossible to know God. God cannot be realized through ostentation and self-conceit. The basic pre-requisite is the shedding of egoism and attachment, so that one can engage oneself in actions with a spirit of detachment. Any person is capable of embarking on this quest without regard to sex, age, caste, or community.

SPIRITUAL DO'S AND DON'TS

The spiritual quest is available to everyone according to his or her capacity and aspirations. However, certain rules and obligations have been laid down for observance by everyone. There are four categories, and all four are obligatory for everyone:

1. *Naimithika Karmas*
2. *Kamya Karmas*
3. *Nishiddha Karmas*
4. *Prayaschitta Karmas*

Naimithika Karmas: These are ritual duties to be carried out with practical actions related to the performance of certain vows, or special ceremonies, during specific periods, or special occasions. Ritual and funeral and ceremonies carried out during an eclipse; all fall into this category. These are obligatory for those leading a family life.

Kamya Karmas: These relate to *Karmas* (rituals) performed for the achievement of specific objectives like seasonal rains, abundance of crops, relief from famine, domestic happiness, peace in society, or attaining Heaven. All karmas done for the sake of securing happiness here and hereafter, are *Kamya Karmas.* All the prayers that are offered for the good of one's family, or the world, are in this category. When the prayers are offered with a pure heart, Divine Grace manifests Itself.

Nishiddha Karmas: These relate to acts which are to be avoided. For instance, the spiritual aspirant must observe certain regulations regarding food. He must totally avoid *Rajasic* food like alcoholic drinks and meat. The nature of food determines the nature of one's thoughts, feelings, and actions. If one's conduct is to be right and proper, one should carefully observe the disciplines regarding diet. To have pure thoughts, one should take only *Sathwic* food. It should be moderate and wholesome. Avoiding unwholesome and impure food is like clearing a field of weeds, so that the crop can grow well. The taboos regarding food have to be observed strictly, so that one's life may be cleansed of all impurities.

Prayaschitha Karmas: These karmas must be done purely to obtain pardon for offences committed either knowingly, or unknowingly. The ancient sages prescribed these practices as a result of their experiences, and the benefit and solaces they derived from practicing them. Experimenting with different practices, they indicated those which were most beneficial and necessary. These include pilgrimages to holy shrines, and bathing in sacred rivers:

'Darsanam papanasanam, Sambhashanam sankata nasanam' (seeing sacred places destroys sin, and conversing with saints, wipes out worries).

People should undertake pilgrimages to holy places from time to time, to get mental peace, and to purify the heart. Such journeys should be made with pure minds, and genuine devotion, without seeking any rewards. Some people enter into curious bargains with the Lord. To make trivial offerings to God to secure large benefits, is a mockery of devotion. There is something very precious in every person. It is his heart. This is what must be offered to the Lord. Standing in the midst of the *Ganga,* the *Krishna,* or *Godavari rivers,* people make offerings to the water to *Keshava, Krishna, or Narayana,* as if they are offering something of their own to the Lord! The very idea that they are offering something is itself misconceived. If people cultivate purity of heart, the Lord will take care of everything, like a mother who attends to every need of the infant.

ATMA JNANA
THE KNOWLEDGE OF THE SOUL

It is the realization of the unity underlying all diversity which constitutes:

Atma-Jnana (knowledge of the Self). It is important to know well and understand well the declaration of the *Upanishads*: *Isavasyam idam sravam* (everything is permeated by God) *Iswara-sarvabhoothanam* (God dwells in all beings)

Many people verbally accept these statements and even preach them, but in practice they promote divisions and differences. Some go as far as betraying God, but it is not in fact God that is betrayed. They are only betraying themselves and giving a false impression of their real selves.

Yagnas and Yagas are performed to invoke the blessings of God for the peace and wellbeing of the Universe. When God responds with His Grace, the wellbeing of all is guaranteed. The Yajnas have yet another significance. Offering to the Lord what he has given to man is a basic duty of the spiritual seeker. The offering is to be regarded not as sacrificing something, but as an act of love and gratitude, in which one rejoices.

The individual should cultivate a generosity of spirit and serve society, regarding it as a manifestation of God Himself. Peace in the world depends upon peace among individuals. The individual, the community, and the world are intimately inter-related. The individual must discover within himself the secret of inner peace and joy which lies within everyone. This joy must be extended to the entire community in which he lives. From the community, it should then expand out to the entire world. The *Gita* declares: *Adveshta Sarvabhoothanam* (*Do not harm any living being*). This should be the guiding principle for every-one. It is to promote this feeling of universal sympathy, that the former *sages* created the *Yagas and Yajnas.*

Bhagavan Sri Sathya Sai Divine Discourse in the
Poorna Chandra Auditorium October 6th, 1986.

22

THE DIVINE LIFE

A convention like that of the workers of the '*Mission of Divine Life*', must embrace all of mankind. All are part of it without exception, and all move painfully on the path of the realization of the immanent divinity. The mission of the human being is to be grounded in the Absolute Existence, where *Sath* (truth), was engendered by the source of all; that is to say, *Brahman*. Equally, *Chith*, (consciousness) is born from the Supreme Consciousness of *Brahman*, and also from *Ananda* (bliss). You are all *Sath-Chit-Ananda*; incarnations of the Supreme Principle, but you are not aware of this. You imagine that you are an individual, subject to this or that limitation. This is the myth that must be abolished to begin a divine life. It is God who inspires, animates, and directs the life of all beings, regardless of their physical struc-ture. All entities, from the smallest to the largest, will one day or another flow into the estuary to merge into the ocean of bliss.

Divine Life is the very breath of all beings. It is *Sathya* (truth), *Prema* (love) and *Ahimsa* (non-violence).

How can one be false to someone, when in reality there is only one person? It is fear that breeds lies. When one realizes that there is only one single entity, there can be no room for such feelings. The entity you love the most in the world is yourself! When you recognize that all that exists, and all human beings, are just another form of you, you can love perfectly. Who could harm whom . . . when all are one?

How to lead a divine life? Any effort to realize the unity at the basis of the apparent multiplicity, is a step towards divine life. You have to churn the milk, if you want to separate and identify the butter that is inherent in it. So, you must go through a certain process of thought and action, to get to the heart of faith. This faith will make you understand that this world is in fact a strange mixture of *Sathyam* (Truth), and of *A-Sathyam* (Non-Truth) and that it is *Mithya* (unreal). Divine life does not allow impurity of character, nor error of judgment. People who live in this way should emphasize their superior qualities, in order to be examples to others.

When the roots of anxiety, fear and ignorance have been pulled out, the true personality of man can be revealed. Faith eliminates anxiety and assures us that whatever happens is for the best, and that the Lord's will must be done. The best armor against anxiety is a quiet acceptance of whatever happens. Sorrow arises from selfishness, from the feeling in life that no one wants to help you. When that egoism that you do not deserve to be so mistreated disappears, sorrow also vanishes. Ignorance is an error, that makes you identify with your physical body.

You have to eliminate your ego completely, and the Lord will use you as a musical instrument. One day I asked a group of people what they would like to see in the hands of God. All of them gave me a different response. Each person told me: The *Lotus,* the *Sanska,* the *Chakra* (different attributes of the Lord when represented in form) etc. but no one has spoken of the flute (the *Murali*) and that the Lord will come, take you, carry you to his lips and blow on your soul. From the bottom of your purified heart, and without trace of ego will arise a sweet melody, which will enchant everything he has created. Be firm, melt your will into His, breathe His Breath, this is True Divine Life. I want everyone to be successful in this path.

Bhagavan Sri Sathya Sai Baba's Discourse
at Venkatagiri: April 1957

There is no one to know who I am, until I created the world for my pleasure with one word. Immediately mountains rose up, immediately rivers started running, earth below, sky overhead, oceans, seas, lands and watersheds, sun, moon, desert sands sprang up from no where, to prove My existence. Then came all forms, human beings, beasts and birds, hearing, speaking, flying. The first place was granted to Mankind and My knowledge was placed in Man's mind.

— BABA

There is No One to Know Who I Am, Until I Created the World for My Pleasure with One Word. Immediately Mountains Rose Up, Immediately Rivers Started Running, Earth Below, Sky Overhead, Oceans, Desert Sands Sprang Up from Nowhere, Seas, Lands and Watersheds, Sun, Moon, to Prove My Existence. Then Came All Forms, Human Beings, Beasts and Birds, Hearing, Speaking, Flying. The First Place Was Granted to Mankind and My Knowledge was Placed in Man's Mind.

23

SAI MAHAVAKHYAS

SOME GREAT REVELATIONS OF
SRI SATHYA SAI BABA

"Walk on this earth, your head held high, your heart open, ready to love, believe in yourself, and in the God who is in you, and all will be well. Wherever you go, I am here. Whoever you contact, I am in that person. I am in everything, and in each of you all. From each I will answer. You cannot see Me only in one place and not see Me in another, because I fill the whole Cosmos! You cannot escape Me, or do anything in secret . . ."

"Do not try to measure Me, you will only fail. Instead, try to discover your measure, and then you will have a better chance of succeeding in understanding My Measure."

"I am not engaged in any asceticism; I don't do any meditation; I don't do any studies; I am neither a yogi nor an ascetic; I have come to guide and bless all the faithful. I am neither man, nor woman, neither young, nor old. I am all of these. Do not praise Me. I love that you approach Me fearlessly and as if it were a right. You don't praise your father, you ask him something as a right, don't you? I do not come into this world uninvited. Ascetics, Saints, Sages, good men of all creeds and all places have called, prayed and begged Me, so I have come. You may be seeing Me for the first time today, but you are all very old connections to Me. I know you through and through. I have neither tendencies (*Gunas*), nor causes (*Karanas*). How then can illusion reach Me?

If I had incarnated as in mythology with the Conch, the Wheel, the Mace, or the Lotus, you would have run away, or you would have placed me in an exhibition. If I had been like one of you, you wouldn't have paid any attention to Me. This is why I have assumed this human form, and I show you these "*Miracles*" from time to time. My task is to bring about the spiritual rebirth of humanity, by means of truth and love. I have come to show you both the way of virtue, and the way to God. If you take one step towards Me, I take three towards you. I am happiest when someone carrying a heavy burden of suffering comes to Me, for they are in great need of what I have to give them. You are all Mine by the kinship of Soul. Those who revere Me are no closer to Me than others . . ."

"It is My Will which leads each of you to come and listen to Me in this place. I am not excluding anyone, any being, this is impossible for Me, it is not in My Nature to do so. Do not be afraid. I Am yours; You are mine."

"You are the invincible Soul, insensitive to the ups and downs of life. The shadow you cast, as you trudge along the road, falls on dirt and dust, bushes and heather, sand and stones, you are not at all worried, because you are walking in safety and health, so therefore, as a soul reality, you have no reason to worry about the fate of your shadow, your body"

"My Mission is to give you courage and joy, to cast out fear and weakness . . . Do not condemn yourself as a sinner, the term sin is incorrect for what is a mistake. I will forgive you all your mistakes, if you sincerely repent, and resolve not to return to sin. Pray to the Lord for the strength to overcome the bad habits that seduced you, while you were in ignorance."

WHAT YOU NEED TO KNOW

"You must know that . . . I Am in you and for you. You are in Me and for Me. But I still have to tell you a little about Me and guide you. You cannot have Me by adulation, and you do not lose Me by denunciation. You have Me by truth, purity, and sincerity. I have come dressed in this human apparatus, to support this truth, the truth of you all.

I am the Truth of Truths, the Truth in all Truths. This Form of *Sai* bears the Name *Truth*. You may have wondered, why did the Truth come to earth in human form? Well, to plant in the Heart of Man this thirst for truth, to put him on the path of truth, to help him reach the goal, the truth, through education, and finally through enlightenment."

**I AM YOU; YOU ARE ME,
ALL ONE, ALL GOD**

"The greatest wealth one can desire is the Grace of God. It will protect you as the eyelids protect the apple of your eye . . ."

"Above all, try to gain Divine Grace, by reforming your bad habits, reducing your desires, and developing what is nobler and higher in you. Each step makes the next easier; this is the best way to progress on the spiritual path. With each step your power and your confidence increases, as do your chances of gaining the Grace of God"

"Personal effort and Divine Grace are interdependent. Without effort, no grace is possible, and without grace, effort does not succeed. To earn this grace, you simply have to have faith and be righteous"

"When you've done your best, and it turns out that it's not enough, then call me; I am always ready to support your efforts by My Grace"

"If one has a pure heart, and lives according to Swami's Teachings, Swami's Grace is automatic. No karma can prevent this"

"I must also speak to you about the importance of Love. Love is God and God is Love. God can only be known and realized, reached, and won, through Love."

"Love is God, God is Love. Love more and more people, Love them intensely. Turn Love into service, turn Service into Devotion. This is the highest spiritual practice."

"Cultivate Love for all; this is the best way to get close to God. I am not measuring distance in terms of kilometers. It is the extent of your Heart, of your Love, which, for me, decides the distance . . ."

MANASE BHAJARE

Manasa Bhajare Guru Charanam
Dustara Bhava Sagara Taranam
Guru Maharaj Guru Jai Jai
Sainatha Sadguru Jai Jai
Sathya Sainatha Sadguru Jai Jai
Om Namah Shivaya, Om Namah Shivaya
Om Namah Shivaya, Shivaya Namah Om,
Arunachala Shiva, Arunachala Shiva
Arunachala Shiva, Aruna Shivom
Omkaram Bhava, Omkaram Bhava
Omkaram Bhava, Om Namo Baba
Meaning: O Mind! Meditate on the Lotus Feet of the Lord.
That Will Take You Safely Across the Ocean of Life and Death.
Glory to the Supreme Guru, Lord Sathya Sai.
Surrender to Lord Shiva, the One who resides in Arunachala.
Bow to Sai Baba, who is Om personified.

The first message *Bhagavan Sri Sathya Sai Baba* gave humankind was "*Manasa Bhajare Guru Charanam, Dusthara Bhava Sagara Tharanam*" meaning:

"*Meditate in thy spirit on the Feet of the Guru. This can take you across the difficult sea of existence in birth after birth.*"

Baba sang this as a boy of 14, and thus declared His Mission of leading humanity back to its connection with the Cosmic Creator. He had returned home from school, and He threw away His books saying:

"*Illusion has left me. I am no longer yours. My devotees are waiting for me.*"

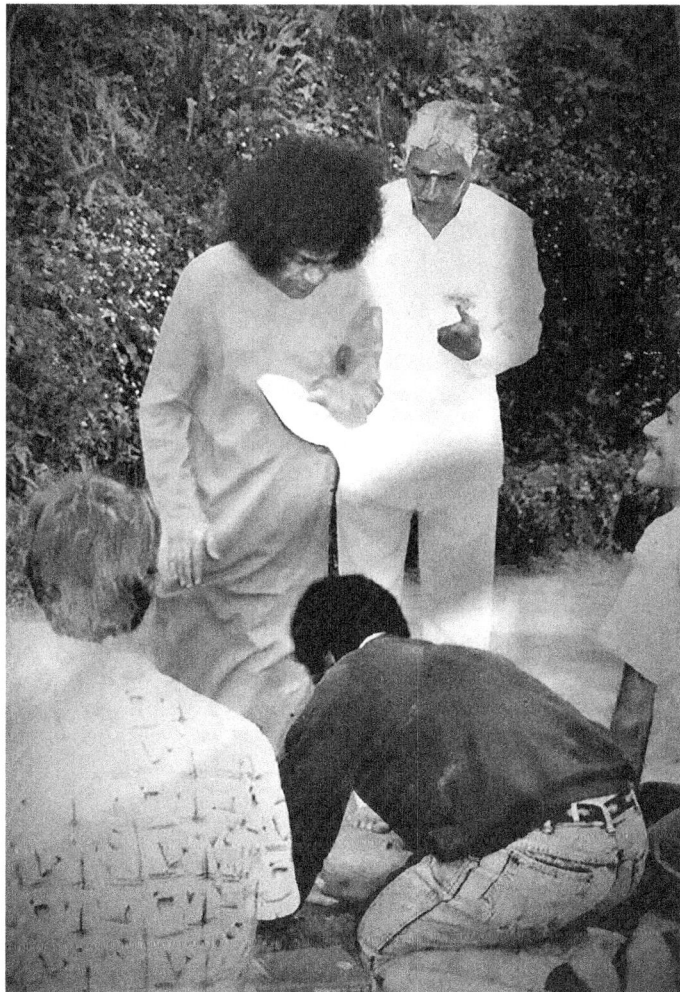

*Padnamaskar – Baba's Divine
Blessing at Ooty May 1988*

GLOSSARY

Meanings of some of the most important Sanskrit words are listed here to help you understand the specific meanings and detailed explanations of terms used in discourses by *Bhagavan Sri Sathya Sai Baba.* I have referred to *Sri Sathya Sai Speaks* for this glossary, for the benefit of lay readers who are interested in Hindu religion and teaching, and for all to better understand what *Baba* was communicating. You will note that there may be additional 'a' letters in many of these Sanskrit words, which are not as commonly used in spellings in modern times. I hope you will find this glossary helpful.

Aananda – Divine Bliss. The Self is unalloyed, eternal bliss. Pleasures are but its faint and impermanent shadows.

Aaraadhana – Divine service, propitiation.

Aakaasha – Space, ether, the subtlest form of matter.

Abhayaswarupam – Fearlessness embodied, of nature of fear-lessness. *Brahman* is fearless.

Adwaitha – non-dualism. The philosophy of absolute oneness of God, Soul and Universe.

Aham Brahmaasmi – "I am *Brahman*". This is one of the great Vedic dicta (*Mahaa Vaakyaas*).

Ahamkaara – Egotism resulting from the identification one's Self with the body. It causes the sense of "I do" and 'I experience".

Ajnaana – Ignorance (which represents perception of the reality).

Annamaya Kosa – Material of gross sheath of the soul, the physical body.

Antharyaamin – Inner Motivator or controller. God is described thus because he resides in all beings and controls them from within.

Archana – ritual worship of a deity, making offerings with recitation of *mantras* and holy names.

Atma – Self, Soul. Self with limitations, is the individual soul (or *Jiva*) Self, with no limitations, is *Brahman*, the supreme reality.

Atma-Jnaana – knowledge of the Self which is held out as the supreme goal of human endeavor.

Atmaswarupam – Self embodied, of the nature of the Self. The real one within us is the Self which is pure consciousness.

Atma Thatwa – principle of the Self, the truth, or the essential nature of the Self.

Avatar – Incarnation of God. Whenever there is a decline of *Dharma*, God comes down to the World assuming bodily form to protect the good, punish the wicked and re-establish *Dharma*. An Avatar is born and lives free and is ever conscious of His Mission. By His precept and example, He opens new paths in spirituality, shedding His Grace on all.

Bhagavatham – A sacred book composed by sage *Vyasa* dealing with *Vishnu* and His incarnations, especially *Sri Krishna*.

Bhajana – Group worship by devotees with devotional music in which repetition of holy names predominates.

Bhagavatham-Thatwam – The truth or essential nature of the Lord.

Bhakta – a devotee who has intense selfless love for God.

Bhakti – devotion to God, intense selfless love for God.

Bhavasaagaram – Ocean of worldly life. The worldly life of a being is considered to be the ocean which he has to cross and reach the other side for liberation from the cycle of birth and death.

Bodha – Perception, knowledge, consciousness.

Bhoga – Enjoyment, experience, the antithesis of yoga.

Buddhi – Intellect, intelligence, faculty of discrimination.

Brahma – The Creator. The first of the Hindu Trinity.

Brahmachari – A celibate student who lives with and learns from his spiritual guide.

Brahmaandham – The Cosmic egg, the Universe.

Brahman – The Supreme Being, the Absolute Reality, Impersonal God with no form or attributes. The uncaused cause of the Universe. Existence, Consciousness, Bliss, Absolute, (*Sath-chith-aanada*), The Eternal Changeless Reality, not conditioned by time, space, and causation.

Dama – Self-control. Restraining the sense organs which run after sense objects seeking pleasure. This is an important discipline for an aspirant practicing yoga.

Dharma – Righteousness, religion, code of duties, duty, essential nature of a being or thing. It holds together the entire Universe.

Man is exhorted to practice *Dharma* to achieve material and spiritual welfare. The *Vedas* contain the roots of *Dharma*. God is naturally interested in the reign of *Dharma*.

Dhyaana – Meditation, an unbroken flow of thought towards the object of concentration. It steadies and stills the mind and makes it fir for realization in course of time.

Dwaitha – Dualism, the doctrine that the individual and the Supreme Soul are two distinct principles.

Gayathri Mantra – The very sacred *Vedic* prayer for Self-enlightenment, repeated piously at dawn, noon, and twilight devotions.

Guna – Quality, property, trait, one of the three constituents of Nature.

Guru – Spiritual guide, a knower of *Brahman*, who is calm, desireless, merciful and ever ready to help and guide the spiritual aspirants who approach him.

Hridayaakasa – Space in the Spiritual heart in which the Self is imagined in meditation and prayer.

Istha Devatha – The chosen Deity through which a devotee contemplates on God.

Iswara – The Supreme Ruler. The personal God. He is *Brahman* associated with *Maaya* but has it under His control unlike the *Jiva*, who is *Maaya*'s slave. He has a lovely Form, auspicious attributes, and infinite power to create, sustain and destroy. He dwells in the heart of every being, controlling it from within. He responds positively to true devotion and sincere prayer.

Japam – Pious repetition of Holy name or sacred *mantra*, practised as a spiritual discipline.

Jiva-Jivaathma – The individual soul in a state of non-realization of its identity with *Brahman*. It is the self-deluded, bound spirit, unaware of its own true nature. It is subjected to sensations of pain and pleasure, birth, and death etc.

Jnaanam – Sacred knowledge of the spirit, pursued as a means to Self-realization. It is direct experience of God, as the Soul of the Souls. *Jnaanam* makes a man omniscient, free, fearless, and immortal.

Jnaani – A sage possessing *Jnaanam* (unitive spiritual knowledge and experience).

Kaarana Sariram – Causal body which carries the impressions and tendencies in seed state. It is the sheath of bliss, the innermost of the five sheaths of the soul.

Karma – Action, deed, work, religious rite, the totality of innate tendencies formed as a consequence of acts done in previous lives. Every *Karma* produces a lasting impression on the mind of the doer apart from affecting others. Repetition of a particular *Karma* produces a tendency (*vaasana*) in the mind. *Karma* is of three kinds. 1. The *Praarabdha*, which is being exhausted in the present life, 2. *The Agami,* which is being accumulated in the present life and 3. *The Samchita,* which is stored to be experienced in future lives.

Kosas – The five sheaths enclosing the soul-sheaths of bliss, intelligence, mind, vital energy, and physical matter.

Kshatriya – A member of the warrior caste, one of the four social groups (*varnas*) of the Hindu community.

Kshetra – field, the body in which the Jiva reaps the harvest of his *karma*.

*Kshetragn*a – The knower of the field, the Spirit, the individual knowing Self.

Leela – Sport, play, the Universe is viewed as Divine Sport or play.

Lingam – Sign, symbol.

Linga Sariram – The subtle body with its vital principles, subtle organs, mind, intellect, and ego. When the gross body dies, the Self departs clothed in the subtle body.

Loka – Any of the 14 worlds (visible and invisible) inhabited by living beings.

Maaya – The mysterious, creative, and delusive power of *Brahman* through which God projects the appearance of the Universe. *Maaya* is the material cause and *Brahman* is the efficient cause of the Universe. *Brahman* and *Maaya* are inextricably associated with each other lie fire and its power to heat. *Maaya* deludes the *Jivas* in egoism, making them forget their true spiritual nature.

Mahabharata – The Hindu epic composed by Sage *Vyasa* which deals with the deeds and fortunes of the cousins (the *Kauravas* and the *Pandavas*) of the Lunar race, with *Lord Krishna* playing a significant and decisive role in shaping the events. The *Bhagavad Gita* and *Vishnu Sahasranama* occur in this great epic. It is considered to be the fifth Veda by devout Hindus. Of this great epic, it is claimed that "what is not in it is nowhere"

Manas – Mind, the inner organ which has four aspects; 1. *Manas* (Mind) which deliberates desires and feels, 2. *Buddhi* (Intellect) that understands, reasons, and decides, 3. *Ahamkaara* ('I' sense) and 4. *Chitha* (Memory). The Mind with all its desires and their broods, conceals the divinity within Man. Purification of the Mind is essential for Realization of the Self.

Maanava – Man, descendent of Manu, the Lawgiver.

Manomaya – *Kosa* – Mental Sheath. One of the five sheaths enclosing the Soul. It consists of the mind and the five subtle sensory organs. It is endowed with the power of will.

Mantra – A sacred formula, mystic, syllable, or word symbol uttered during the performance of rituals or meditation. They represent the spiritual truths directly revealed to the *Rishi's* (Seers). The section of the *Veda* which contains these hymns (*mantras*) is called the *Samhitha.*

Moksha/Mukthi – Liberation from all kinds of bondage, especially the one to the cycle of birth and death. It is a state of absolute freedom, peace, and bliss, attained through Self-realization. This is the supreme goal of human endeavor, the other three being, *Dharma* (Righteousness), *Artha* (wealth and power) and *Kaama* (sense-pleasure).

Naamasmarana – Remembering God through His name, one of the most important steps of spiritual discipline (*Saadhana*) to obtain God's Grace and to make progress in the spiritual journey.

Nididhyaasana – Concentration on the truth about the Self after hearing it (*Sravana* from the Guru and reflecting on it (*Manama*). It is thus the third step on the path of Knowledge (*Jnaana* – Yoga).

Nivrithi Marga – The path of renunciation that demands giving up desires and concentrating on God. The *Upanishads* which form the *Jnaana-Kanda* (the section dealing with unitive spiritual knowledge) of the *Vedas*, deal with this path. This path is opposed to the *Pravrithi Marga* (the path of desire) which worldly men pursue, seeking the good things here and hereafter.

Praanamaya Kosa – Sheath of vital energy. It consists of five vital principles and five subtle organs of action. It is endowed with the power of action.

Prakrithi – Nature, The Divine Power of Becoming, also known as *Maaya, Avidya* and *Sakthi*, the world of matter and mind as opposed to the Spirit. *Prakrithi* has three dispositions or *Gunas,* (*Sathwa, Rajas* and *Tamas*) that go into the make-up of all living and non-living beings in the Universe, in varying proportions leading to the appearance of infinite multiplicity in form, nature and behavior.

Pranava – Om – The Sacred Seed Sound and Symbol of *Brahman.* "The most exalted syllable in Vedas". It is used in meditation on God. It is uttered first before a Vedic Mantra is chanted.

Puja – ritual Worship in which a Deity is invoked in an idol or picture and propitiated as a Royal Guest with offerings of flowers, fruits, and other edibles along with recitation of appropriate *mantras* and show of relevant signs.

Puranas – The Hindu *Sastras* (scriptures) in which Vedic truths are illustrated through tales of Divine Incarnations and heroes. *Sage Vyasa* is believed to have written them. Of the 18 *Puranas, Srimad Bhagavatha* is the best known.

Raamayana – This sacred Hindu Epic, composed by *Sage Valmiki* deals with the incarnation of *Vishnu* as *Sri Rama* who strove all His Life to re-establish the reign of *Dharma* in the world. *The Raamayana* has played a very important role in influencing and shaping the Hindu ethos over the centuries.

Rajas/Rajo Guna – One of the three *Gunas* (qualities or dispositions) of *Maaya* or *Prakrithi. Rajas* is the quality of passion, energy, restlessness, attachment, and extroversion. It results in pain.

Thaapam – pain, misery, distress caused by the three types of agencies (*Thaapathrayam*). The agencies are *Aadhyaadmika* (disease and disturbance of body and mind), *Aadhibhowthika* (other beings), and *Aadhi Deivikam* (Supernatural agencies like storm, floods, earthquakes, planets etc

Thamas – One of the *Gunas* (qualities and dispositions) of *Maaya* and *Prakriti.* It is the quality of dullness, inertia, darkness, and tendency to evil. It results in ignorance.

Saadhana – Spiritual discipline or effort aimed at God realization. The *Saadhaka* (aspirant) uses the spiritual discipline to attain the goal of realization.

Samaadhi – it is the super-conscious state transcending the body, mind, and intellect, attained through rigorous and protracted *Saadhana*. In that state of consciousness, the objective world and the ego vanish, and the reality is perceived or communed with, in utter peace and bliss. When in this state, the aspirant realizes his Oneness with God, it is called *Nirvikalpa Samaadhi*.

Samsaara – Worldly life, life of the *Jiva* through repeated births and deaths. Liberation means getting freed from this cycle.

Sanaathana Dharma – Eternal Religion. A descriptive term for what has come to be called Hindusim. It has no single founder or text of its own. It is more a commonwealth of religious faiths and a way of life.

Sastras – The Hindu Scriptures containing the teachings of the *Rishis*. The *Vedas,* the Upanishads, the *Ithihases* (epics), the Puranas and the *Smrithis* (codes of conduct) etc. form the *Sastras* of the Hindus. They teach us how to live wisely and well with all the tenderness and concern of the mother.

Sathwa – One of the three *Gunas* (qualities and dispositions) of *Maaya* or *Prakrithi.* It is the quality of purity, brightness, peace, and harmony. It leads to knowledge. Man is exhorted to overcome *Thamas* by *Rajas* and *Rajas* by *Sathwa,* and finally to go beyond *Sathwa* itself to attain Liberation.

Sthitha Prajna – A man of realization with a steady tranquil and cheerful mind ever dwelling on God. He is a man of self-control, even minded in all circumstances and totally free from all selfish desires. After Death he attains freedom from *Samsaara*.

Swadharma – Ones *Dharma* or duty that accords with one's nature. This is an important concept in the *Gita.*

Upaasana – Worship or contemplation of God.

Upanishad – The very sacred portions of the Vedas that deal with God, man, and universe., their nature and inter-relationships. Spiritual knowledge (*Jnaana*) is their content, so they form the *Jnaana Kaanda* of the Vedas.

Vairagya – Detachment, desire, and ability to give up all transitory enjoyments.

Varnaashrama Dharma – The Hindu community is divided into four *Varnas* (social groups), based on *Gunas* and vocations. Each *Varna* has its own *dharma* (*Varna Dharma*). *Brahmana* is the custodian of spiritual and moral lore. He is the priest and the teacher. The *Kshyatria* rules and defends the land. Trade, agriculture, and cattle rearing are the *Dharmas* of the *Vaisyas*. Labor and service is the Dharma of the Sudhras. The life of a Hindu consists of four stages or *Ashramas* – The student celibate, (*Brahmachari*) the householder (*Grihasta*), the recluse in the forest (*Vaanaprastha*) and the monk (*Sannyasin*).

Vedas – The oldest and the holiest of the Hindu Scriptures, the primary source of authority in Hindu religion and philosophy. They are four in number – The *Rig Veda, Saama Veda, Yajur Veda* and *Atharva Veda*.

Vedantha – Means "the end of the *Vedas*" It is the essence of the *Vedas* enshrined in the *Upanishads.* The philosophy of non-Dualism, or qualified non-Dualism based on the Upanishadic teachings, is denoted by this term.

Vijnaanamaya Kosa – One of the five *Kosas* (Sheaths) of the Soul. It consists of intellect, and the five subtle sense organs. it is endowed with the power to know. The 'I' or subject or experience or action is seated here.

Viveka – Discrimination, the reasoning by which one realizes what is real and permanent and what is non-real and impermanent.

Yagna – A *Vedic* rite or sacrifice. Any self-denying act of service in the name of God.

Yoga – means union with God, as also the path by which this union of the Soul with God is achieved. The four important paths of *Yoga* are those of knowledge, action, meditation, and devotion.

ABOUT THE AUTHOR

ROGER DIGBO

Born in the Ivory Coast, since first receiving *Padnamaskar* with *Baba* in 1988, Roger's life mission has been sharing and spreading the sacred message and teachings of *Bhagavan Sri Sathya Sai Baba*, Divine Avatar of our day (The Incarnation of the Supreme God). Now based in London, Roger is a lifelong spiritual mentor and holistic therapist, who regularly uses reflexology, pressure point treatment, and *Sai Vibrionics* in community service.

With *Baba*'s grace, he promotes spiritual healing, delivers study circles online and offline, and is widely known for his full hearted and uplifting bhajan singing.

Blessed with decades long experience at *Baba*'s Divine Lotus feet, for many years Roger brought large groups of devotees to *Prasanthi Nilayam*, led study programs, and received numerous interviews with *Baba*. A gifted storyteller and speaker, he loves nothing more than to share the priceless words of wisdom and countless wonderful stories based on his own direct personal experiences with *Baba*, so his stories are priceless prasad, for any hungry heart longing to deepen their devotion to *Bhagavan*.

Since the 1990's, Roger has consistently worked in self-less service within the *Sri Sathya Sai Organization*, in the UK, France, and Africa, and he loves to focus on sharing his love for *Baba* with young *Sai* devotees, lighting the lamp of love for generations to come. Roger is also particularly devoted to sharing *Baba*'s strong message of the importance of both *Namasmarana* (reciting the name of God), and chanting the *Gayatri Mantra*, given by *Bhagavan Sri Sathya Sai Baba* for the spiritual protection and advancement of souls everywhere in this critical time of global challenge.

Please visit Roger's new YouTube channel at the link below, and *Like & Subscribe* if you would like to join in his future live events, study circles, and to be kept informed of his ongoing seva and charity work in Africa and the UK.

http://www.youtube.com/@rogerdigbo1618

"Why Fear when I Am here?
I Am always with you, wherever you are,
Protecting you, Guiding you,
Go Forth and Have No fear,
From Love, With Love, In Love

Start the day with Love,
Spend the day with Love,
Fill the Day with Love,
End the Day with Love,
This is the Way to God

Bhagavan Sri Sathya Sai Baba September 1979

Printed in Great Britain
by Amazon